BLACK GIRLS

ABRAMS, NEW YORK

SEW

Projects and Patterns to Stitch and Make Your Own

HEKIMA HAPA and LESLEY WARE

CONTENTS

4. SEW, WHAT'S NEXT?

FOREWORD

by Constance C.R. White

Ouch. I pricked my finger with the needle I was using to hem a jumpsuit. I had borrowed the black-and-white look to wear to New York Fashion Week, and the hemming was an emergency operation I chose because I wanted to send it back as pristine as I had gotten it.

Yes, I know how to sew.

But I'm a novice compared to the jumpsuit's designer and the sky-rocketing number of people now learning to sew by hand or by using sewing machines. The designer and I are both Black women. Fabulous Black women who have flown high with careers in fashion and, speaking for myself, higher than I ever imagined. But right now I had fabric that needed to be turned up. And with my feet firmly on the ground I feel self-sufficient, because I learned to sew when I was a girl.

The unraveled hem could've meant a delay in returning a borrowed garment. It could've meant several hours lost from my already Zoom-filled days and way-too-short nights. I would've had to drop it off, then pick it up from a professional sewer. And when would I get it back? Who knows? But here I was, unbothered, because I know how to sew.

I know how to sew like I know how to jumpstart a dead car battery, or make avocado toast or crispy chicken. You wouldn't have to pay me to do it and it may not always be pretty, but I can get it done. And you'd be grateful.

When you sew, or make some fried chicken, you feel like you've accomplished something. You start to develop a sense of independence and self-realization.

9

I remember quiet, solitary moments of reverie when I first learned how to baste.

Needle in, Needle out.

I learned to do blind hemming, picking out the tiniest thread in the fabric so the stitch would be barely discernible on the outward-facing side. It required the concentration of an Olympic runner steadying herself in the starting blocks.

Learning embroidery, I savored delight as I pulled the thick, colorful threads through the loops in the white tea towels, the stitches forming an artful pattern. When you focus that hard on your craft, you lose yourself in the sweetest way possible. You're enveloped in a feeling of accomplishment and happiness. You did it. You did that.

Sewing was once considered one of the wifely arts, a description that I appreciate is long dead, at least in America. As industrialization brought us mass goods and fast fashion has dubiously made clothes available at lightning speed, the slow, artful process of sewing has ebbed back into the mainstream.

But for Black women, sewing has maintained a pride of place. Perhaps it's because we—out of necessity more than choice—hug up on self-sustenance and creativity. Something that if you sew you know about.

In Black communities isolated by segregation, seamstresses were a fixture alongside the hairstylist, the neighborhood barber, and the local soul food chef. Often the seamstress was someone who today would be called a designer. Sometimes she got little credit for her endeavors. In other cases, Black women built thriving businesses from their ability to sew.

Forced long ago to make our own clothes, we're picking up needle and thread again to make our own creations. Not because we have to, but because we want to.

Around the globe Black girls, and boys, sew, inheriting from women and men in their community the skill to make something from nothing. In cities like Abidjan and Nairobi, I was enthralled to see talented sewers curled over their sewing machines in markets and street stalls, sewing the most beautiful garments. On the other side of town, equally talented creators with more resources displayed their alluring designs in their own elegant boutiques.

Fashion is a more than $2 trillion global industry, and it's rooted in sewing. That's a fact. Yet we don't often enough connect the dots when we watch the models whizzing down the Chanel runway, or see a Gucci bag slung over a woman's (or man's) shoulder, or think about factories pushing out the latest Nike sneakers.

It's not a radical idea to begin sewing for sheer enjoyment and end up running your own company. Or you could have a career behind the scenes as a designer, a seamstress, a sample-maker, or a retailer with mad skills and an uncanny understanding of a garment's fashion and fit.

Black female designers like Tracy Reese, Fe Noel, and Sheila Grey (Byron Lars's partner) use the craft of sewing in their work. Speaking of Lars, while many have drawn or painted their way into fashion, a bunch of them have sewn. Lars, Epperson, Kevan Hall, and Victor Glemaud are among them. Stephen Burrows, the most important Black designer of the last fifty years, said he was inspired by watching his mother sew at their home in New Jersey. Similarly, celebrity stylist Freddie Leiba, who's styled for *Essence*, *Harper's Bazaar*, *Vogue*, *Allure*, and *InStyle*, said his first introduction to fashion was through his mother's sewing.

If mama isn't inspiration enough, we can look at a fistful of robust, pivotal figures in history who were Black sewists.

Elizabeth Keckley's name may not be up there in lights with folks like Maurizio Gucci, but the woman sewed well and was in demand. Her most prominent client was Mary Todd Lincoln, the wife of President Abraham Lincoln.

But Keckley wasn't the only African American to make clothes for a first lady. Anne Lowe, known for her detailed floral embroidering on elaborate gowns, created Jacqueline Bouvier's wedding dress when she married future president John F. Kennedy. And of course, in our lifetimes, there's the gorgeous, ever-slaying Michelle Obama, who's been dressed by Reese, Noel, and Kai Milla.

Beyond this glorious history of sewing there are our valuable contributions to sustainability efforts. As sewers and fashion lovers, Black girls and the African American community are at the forefront of one of the world's most urgent issues, making a healthy planet for long-term survival. Close to eighty percent of the clothes we buy will end up discarded after just a few years, according to one study. Sewing our own wardrobes or home décor is a vote for sustainability and against overproduction.

Thinking about *Black Girls Sew* reminded me of something in me I had long forgotten: To sew is to find a refuge from life's trials and tribulations—from exclusion, times of crises, being misunderstood, growing up, or even growing older.

So why not pick up a needle and thread? Why not engage with this storied craft? Why not learn to make exactly what you want? And if the question for Black girls is: Why me? Then the answer is: Black Girls Sew.

Welcome to the new world of sewists.

INTRODUCTION

Welcome to *Black Girls Sew*! We are so excited for you to join our world of sewing to create your own fashionable, stylish wares. We made this book for you because there's nothing else like it that exists. Inside, you will learn how to make and discover things. You'll uncover new information, find out more about the fashion industry and those who've impacted it, and have some fun along the way.

We hope you will use this book as a starting point for your fashionable aspirations and as an opportunity to keep learning. But most importantly, we want you to enjoy making these projects—because that's what this book is all about.

As sewists ourselves, we know what it can be like in the wide world of fashion. We've had to endure many highs and lows on our journeys through this industry and we wanted to help pave the way to make it more accessible for those who want in. This is the book we wish we'd had, and we hope it's the one that you've been looking for. There is so much personal power in fashion, and we want you to find your lane and keep pushing forward.

Sew, let's go!

HOW TO USE THE BOOK

It's up to you!

You could:

- Read it cover to cover.
- Jump around from chapter to chapter. Maybe you'll want to start in Sew Intentionally (32–33), with sewing basics, or Sew, What's Next? (151–152), to learn about careers in the fashion industry.
- Read it in reverse.
- Read through the different surface technique samples (pages 141–148) before you start sewing.

The most important things to remember as you go along, however you decide to approach this book, are:

- Let go of the fear of messing up.
- Know that customization is the beauty of DIY.
- Daydream and envision what you want.
- Take your time—you're here to have fun.

As we sit in a time perfect for change, the world is truly yours. We want you to get tangled up in the magic of creating your fashion through the projects in this book, and then go further.

Find what's missing, redefine a facet of fashion, make a small shift that leads to a bigger positive change, or just simply enjoy the freedom of creating something unique.

Imagine a world where sewing gives you unlimited joy, energy, and abundance. A place where freedom and the ability to dream are supreme and your highest creative self resides.

Something new is needed, and this is our chance to make it happen. Let's walk toward the fashion future we deserve together.

Visualize it. Believe it. Be here now.

Beautiful Black girl, this book is for you!

1. SEW

CREATIVELY

The creative process is everything. In this chapter, you will learn about the components of a creative process so you can develop your own.

Now is not the time to hold back, but an opportunity to rush forward into the possibilities that await! The creative part is half the fun, *sew* let's get to it.

The creative process is basically the thinking that goes into a project to bring it to life. All artists have different creative processes that can involve collecting inspiration, exploring what inspires them, researching other creatives, carving out a path for their curiosity, and more. It might also include meditation, drawing, mood boarding, and writing, too. But being creative is the key—allowing your brain to move freely from idea to idea, and, when the right one comes along, to run with it. The creative process is important because it will help you to find your way and communicate your genius.

The pages that follow will cover:

- **Mood Boarding**
- **Drawing & Sketching**
- **Studying Color**
- **Note Taking**
- **Creating a Workspace**

Mood Boarding

A mood board is a collection of visuals that evoke a concept or style. Designers, photographers, graphic artists, and others often use mood boards to communicate the look and feel of their ideas and as a personal reference while working on the project. Mood boards are one of the first steps in the creative process, and they can help you to communicate your vision to others. For example, if you are hosting a party, you might want to create a mood board to come up with a scheme for the decorations, food displays, and activities that those helping you get set up can refer to.

The magic in mood boarding is simple: seeing something in a visual format can help you turn it into a reality. Not only are mood boards useful in your planning, they are fun to create and can really jumpstart your creativity.

This is a helpful formula for creating a mood board:

FEELING + VISUAL THEME + MEDIA INSPIRATION

- **Feeling** involves the story that your mood board tells, or the feeling that you want to conjure. For example, freedom and liberation, Afrofuturism, dreamy and nostalgic, or warm and cozy are all ideas that you might want to get across in your work.

- **Visual Theme** involves the colors, tones, and textures that you want to use on your board. For example, black and white, kente cloth colors, or cool muted tones could inform your board.
- **Media Inspiration** calls upon existing movements or time periods that you are inspired by, and uses media references from those periods like newspaper or magazine clippings, movies or TV shows, and news segments. For example, sixties civil rights fashion, Black Girl Magic, Harlem Renaissance, Y2K.

Keeping a notebook with magazine clippings, sketches, or photos of other things you like is a great way to start preparing for a mood board. You can make a physical mood board, design one on a computer, or draw one on paper.

Ideas for what to do with your mood board after you finish:

- Sketch an inspired fashion design (see page 23).
- Create your own custom motif by drawing something you find interesting from the board over and over (and over again).
- Hang it above your desk for inspiration.

We used a mood board in the process of making this book; you can see it on the next page.

you're amazing

BLACK

GIRLS

SEW

Drawing & Sketching

Being able to sketch is very helpful in the creative process of sewing. If you find you struggle with drawing, remember that practice can be the key to unlocking your potential. Grab a notebook or sketchbook, some pencils, and an eraser, and see where your mood board takes you.

Once you're ready to start sketching projects or more concrete ideas, there are numerous tools at your disposal. In particular, for plotting out sewing projects and ideas a croquis is most commonly used. *Croquis* is French for "sketch"; it is also referred to as a template or fashion figure.

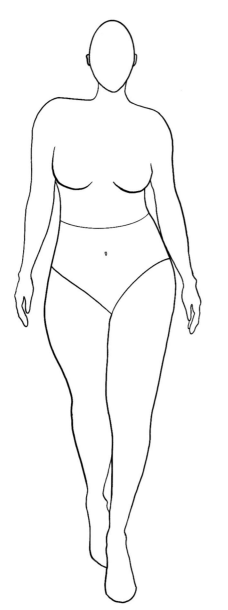

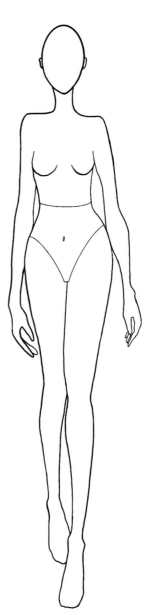

Don't worry about perfection when it comes to drawing. Designers are creators who dance to the beat of their own drum, and as long as you can communicate your ideas through your drawings you're good! So use the croquis outlines on page 23 or draw your own, and start drafting some ideas.

Additional materials you may need for sketching are on page 43.

Once you "dress" your croquis, give it skin tone and a hairstyle, plus details like accessories and a face. Use colored pencils, watercolors, or even makeup, like dark blush that you can smudge onto the paper with your finger, to create skin tone. See the image below to understand the proportions of a face.

When you are sketching, let go of the fear of messing up. Your challenge is to communicate your design ideas best as you can. The more you practice, the better you'll become. We promise it gets easier and easier.

Tip: YouTube is a great resource for inspiration when sketching because you can find anything there. For example, if you want to draw a T-shirt, just search "how to draw a T-shirt" and you will find many easy, step-by-step videos to watch.

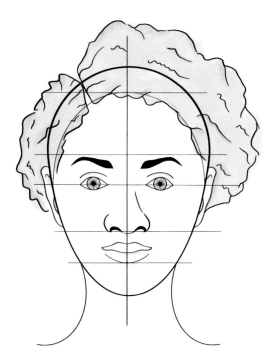

Studying Color

Color is everywhere. It is in our clothing, our homes, at school, and on the streets. Not only do your color choices make a big difference in your final projects, but they're a great way to express yourself. The colors you choose for fashion can be a range, like our skin and like the rainbow. When you're choosing fabrics, from thrifted to upcycled, or making textile prints, study color and make well thought-out choices.

Color has three main functions:

1. Identification of objects
2. The creation of beauty
3. The expression of emotion

We use color to identify people, things, places, land, and sky. Imagine if everything were limited to only black and white, and there were no other colors—how would you be able to tell what was what?

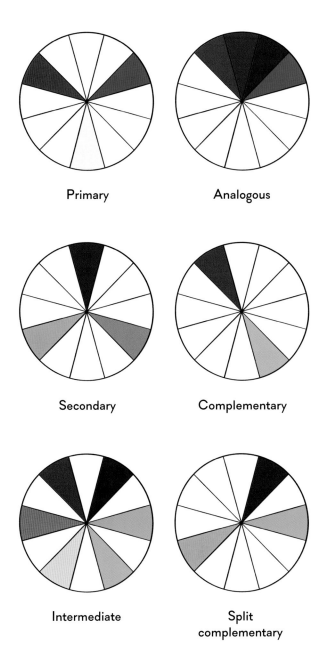

Primary

Analogous

Secondary

Complementary

Intermediate

Split complementary

COLOR THEORY

For all of existence, color has had meaning in different cultures. For example, kente cloth, a Ghanaian textile made of handwoven cloth strips, is not just random colors and shapes mixed to look pretty. Each cloth's pattern has a meaning. The colors and symbols communicate a message about the wearer to the viewer.

Kente comes from the Ghanaian word *kenten*, which means "basket." In the past, the fabric was worn like a toga by royalty among West African tribes. In modern Ghana, kente is more widespread and worn to celebrate special occasions.

The colors we choose to wear can affect our mood and change how we are seen. For example, on days that you want to blend into the scene of NYC many people wear all black, but when you want to stand out or need a mood boost, something like a brightly colored floral or African printed piece is a good way to go.

The list that follows shows different variations of colors, along with some of the symbolism and science associated with each of them.

BLACK: maturation, spiritual energy, spirits of ancestors, power, luxury, seriousness, and mystery.

BLUE: peace, harmony, and love. Blue is a cool color often connected to divinity and truth. It can also be used to express loneliness, aka "the blues." Some different shades of blue include bluebird, aqua, teal, navy, royal, peacock, and Sistine.

GREEN: vegetation, planting, harvesting, growth, spring, and prosperity. It is easy on the eyes. Some shades of green include spring green, emerald, olive, bottle, hunter, moss, kelly, palmetto, and reseda.

GOLD/YELLOW: royalty, wealth, high status, glory, beauty, spiritual purity, and wisdom. Some shades of gold and yellow include lemon, popcorn, leghorn, maize, and tobacco.

PURPLE: sorrow and regality. Lighter purple hues represent delicacy and femininity. Some shades of purple include mauve, lilac, orchard, lavender, plum, and eggplant.

WHITE: purification, joy, glory, and innocence. White can also be associated with death and the afterlife. Some shades of white include eggshell, ivory, ecru, pearl, and off-white.

RED: strength, politics, spirituality, blood, fierceness, love, beauty, happiness, and cheerfulness. Maroon and pink are variations of red—maroon is associated with the color of Mother Earth and healing, while pink is traditionally femme and happy. Some shades of red include rose, fuchsia, cherry, scarlet, paprika, raspberry, and mahogany.

GRAY: serenity, purity, joy; often associated with the moon. Gray is also tied to healing and cleansing rituals; it calls to mind ash. Some shades of gray include silver, smoke, and anthracite.

Have you ever heard of reseda or ecru? If not, or if there are any other colors you haven't heard of before, be sure to look them up to get a visual for their different hues. Having an exact color in mind when shopping for fabric and items to upcycle will help you execute your final project.

Study color and get a sense of what works well together, but remember to always wear the colors that make you feel good. In the past, some put parameters around dressing in color according to age, size, occasion, or skin color, but we no longer need to be restricted this way. For example, in the eighties women in the workforce usually wore "power suits" in dark colors like brown, black, or navy— conservative colors, because they wanted to be taken seriously by their male counterparts. And the days of baby girls wearing pink and baby boys wearing blue are long gone. Color should make you feel confident, so find your own power color and own it!

Tip: You can test fabric colors before you try them out for flyness by placing them over your shoulder to see what is most becoming. Collect several pieces of fabric and bring them along next time you are with friends. Experiment to see what colors look best on one another. Take notes in your journal (see page 30).

Hidden Figure of Fashion:

BERNADINE M. ANDERSON

(1942–)

Bernadine M. Anderson was Hollywood's first Black female makeup artist. During her twenty-year career, she worked on several films, including classics like *Coming to America, Boomerang, What's Love Got to Do with It, Another 48 Hours,* and the television series *Roots.* Due to Bernadine's talent, she was requested by various members of the Black Stuntmen's Association to make their faces mimic the main actor they were standing in for. She often shaped the looks of the stunt doubles and even triples who stood in for the primary actor.

Bernadine was "blessed," as she says in a video from 2012, to be offered an apprenticeship at Warner Brothers, which opened up her career.

The apprenticeship sharpened her talent and led to her being a highly sought-after makeup artist for celebrities working in film, including the legendary Cicely Tyson. She was even requested by "it girl" Jane Fonda in the sixties, a time when Black makeup artists did not work on white films. She also dabbled as an artist for blaxploitation films, including *Trouble Man* and *Black Girl.*

In the seemingly glamorous world of makeup artistry, Bernadine had to be bold and break barriers. For example, after being unfairly denied work, she filed—and won—a class-action lawsuit to be accepted into the Local 706 Make-Up Artists & Hairstylists Guild.

In 2015, Jane Fonda presented Bernadine with the Outstanding Achievement in Makeup at the Hollywood Beauty Awards. Her original makeup kit can be seen on display at the Smithsonian National Museum of African American History and Culture.

Bernadine is a queen for demanding the right to be in places where Black women were told they should not be seen.

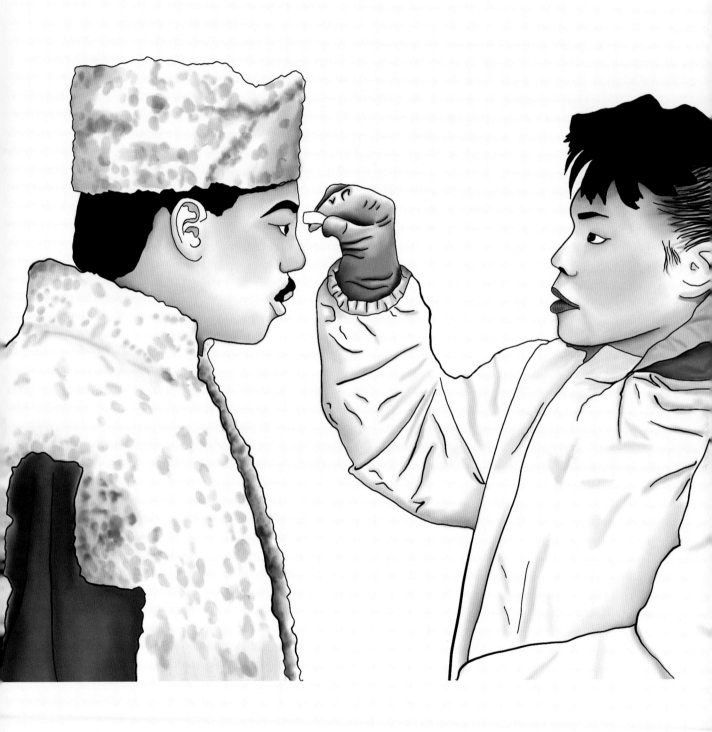

Note Taking

Taking notes might seem old-fashioned, but it can be your secret weapon. As you are sketching, sewing, and designing, grab a journal to take notes, draw, doodle, or create symbols in. When you make clear notes about your projects, you can review them later and have a better understanding of the process of putting your work together. (You should see how many notes we took while writing this book!)

After you finish your sewing projects, reflection is a good idea. Write down your thoughts about the project, and how you feel now that it's complete.

- How do you feel about the finished piece?
- How could it be improved?
- Were there any surprises along the way?
- What did you learn from this project?
- What will you do differently next time (size of the project, fabric choice, embellishments, etc.)?
- How can you adapt this project to be more sustainable?

Creating a Workspace

Talk to your household about transforming a corner, a small table, or a closet into your sewing workspace. Having a small sewing studio will make it easier for you to take time to be creative. Consider elements like colors and smells. For instance, you may want to decorate with photos or fabrics, or maybe plants or flowers to bring nature into the space. Every workplace can benefit from music, so find inspiration in a fun playlist. Make a sewing playlist of ten or more songs—lo-fi hip-hop beats stations

are cool if you want a chill, ambient, focused vibe, or maybe you play your favorite artist on repeat. Your space; your way! (See what we love listening to on pages 163 and 165.)

Ideas to consider for your studio space:

- What type of lighting do you like? Maybe you want a soft white bulb instead of one that casts yellow light, or maybe you place your workspace next to a window. Natural light is amazing.
- What sewing resources do you need to reference? In addition to this book, what other books will you keep about sewing, fashion, and design on your bookshelf? If you have a sewing machine, you will also want to keep your sewing manual handy along with your fashion journal.
- What textures and fabrics do you like? Bring materials into your space to create art with. How can you use your fabric scraps to make a mural? Can you hang clothing on the wall for inspiration?
- What are the quotes, images, or affirmations that motivate you? Consider setting a ritual, like saying an affirmation or visualizing something positive before you start to create.
- How will you keep your space tidy? Consider your clean up after crafting and sewing. What things need to be put away? What will you leave out? What needs to be unplugged (glue guns, sewing machines, iron, etc.)? Note: If you have pets, make sure you clean up any pins, needles, or sharp objects with care. You don't want your best friend to accidentally get hurt. If possible, keep your pets out of your workspace.

MAKE YOUR OWN AFFIRMATION!

Affirmations are a great way to remind yourself of your set goals and ambitions. Craft your own that speaks to your aims, and recite it when you begin a new project, are feeling stuck creatively, or just need a little boost in your mood.

Affirmations are always composed in the first person, and they are actionable. Yours could be, "I imagine myself in a resource-rich environment that supports and honors my creativity." Or it could be, "I amplify my voice in a space that embraces, welcomes, and makes room for me." Whatever you want to get back from the universe, you should put out into it!

Tapping into your Black Girl Magic happens when you are surrounded by inspiring things. Place your affirmation on your wall and recite it before you sew. Sit with yourself and feel what it means.

Tip: Dig into your family's history to better understand what fashion was like for your ancestors. If you can, go back in history to the 1970s, 1960s, 1950s, or further. Find photos, ask questions of the oldest person from your family, do regional research, and use your imagination.

You have to know where you've been to go further. Period. We *are* because they *were*. And you can be more!

2. SEW

INTENTIONALLY

A Brief History of Sustainable Fashion & Textiles

As much fun as sewing and the world of fashion can be, there are some deeper issues within the textile industry that we as consumers and creators should be aware of. The truth is, sustainable fashion is rooted in Black history in the United States. Long before it was a trend, Black people wore hand-me-downs, mended up old clothes, and made new pieces from existing garments. As enslaved people forced into this country, we dressed modestly out of necessity.

The textile industry, also known as the first great industry, was built on the labor and skills of Black people. In school, many have learned about the cotton gin, an invention of Eli Whitney in 1793. Separating cotton from seeds, this new machine could make cotton useable much more quickly, and it turned cotton crops into cash during the industrial revolution, enabling the mass production of fabric across the globe. The history books seem to have glossed over the fact that as the demand for cotton grew, so did the need for slave labor. This factor resulted in an increase in punishment from slave owners and made for even more harsh working environments for enslaved Africans.

Another traditionally used fabric was fur. You may not have heard quite as much about this, but so much of North American history is wrapped up in fur. Beaver fur was one of the first imports that was very popular in places like New York in the 1600s. By 1730, the Hudson's Bay Company, now Saks Fifth Avenue, was exporting more than 39,000 beaver pelts a year, and by 1836 beavers were almost extinct. In the mid-1900s, many stars, including opera singer Marian Anderson and singer Billie Holiday, dressed in fur to perform, and companies would give Black stars fur coats as part of campaigns to help them sell more, mostly because Black women styled the coats in unique ways. As the use of fur coats and accessories in popular culture increased, companies understood that they could sell more if they marketed to Black people, because we had been excluded from this luxe outerwear in the past. Now we're seeing more and more companies and fashion houses move away from fur, as fashion continues to move in a more sustainable direction. And Black people are again at the forefront of this change.

There is an unbreakable bond between Black people, sustainable fashion, and cotton that still plays out today. We share this to point out that Black people have existed in fashion forever, in every way, right from the start, but we have not been recognized for the value we inherently bring. Black spending tops the charts in fashion and beauty, and often we are just seen as consumers, but the truth is we are so much more.

Fashion is so important to us now because it was not always accessible. During certain periods of American history, Black people were poor and marginalized in many different ways.

For example, we could not shop at the same places as our white counterparts. What we wear now can be seen as a symbol, and having the *freshest gear* removes some of the sting of prior struggles, but it cannot erase the past.

As we saw with Bernadine M. Anderson, profiles that highlight Black fashion heroes are sprinkled throughout the book. These are informative biographies of mostly female fashion pioneers (with the exception of visionary Patrick Kelly) who broke barriers and found their own paths despite the challenges they faced. We hope that you will be inspired by their stories. Maybe one will serve as a road map as you come into your own fashion future.

Green fashion is always top of mind at Black Girls Sew. We have a program called Sew Green because sustainability starts with all of us. Maybe you pride yourself on being ahead of the game and like new things, but you want to figure out how to do this in a green way. Everything does not have to be brand new; in fact, buying secondhand and repurposing secondhand clothes or bed linens and curtains to keep something new is a great way to make your fashion sustainable. As you begin to collect or purchase the materials needed for the projects, keep in mind what the material is (natural or synthetic) and how the fabric needs to be cared for (hand wash, machine friendly, or dry clean only). If you have leftovers, can you reuse them for a future project? If you are upcycling, read the label inside to see where the garment was made. Can you research the company to find out if they are transparent about their production process?

Now that you have some backstory and some ideas for how to work sustainability into your fashionable future, let's get started with supplies to create that future. Who knows, you might create the next new hot trend, expanding fashion into places where it has never been.

The power is in your hands!

In this book we will show you how to choose upcycled materials like scraps, thrifted clothing, and deadstock (materials that would otherwise be thrown away) to maximize the green factor in your sewing projects.

3. SEW

PATTERNS

SEWING PATTERNS

It's time to sew! We're going to make a few practical (and outrageous) clothing items and accessories. This is a chance for you to discover your style. Once you learn the basics, you can take your sewing to the next level by putting your own spin on it!

At the end of the chapter, you will find additional surface design and embellishment techniques to try. They will help you when you are ready to redesign a pattern and make it again.

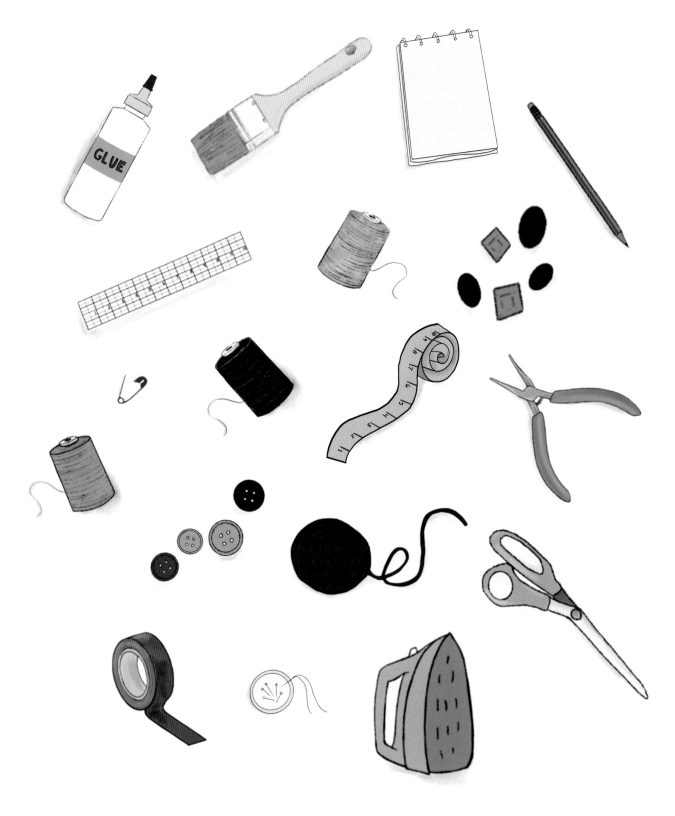

Basic Tools & Materials

These are some general materials and tools that you will need to complete the projects in this book.

FOR DRAWING

- Pencil
- Colored pencils
- Clear ruler (you will also use this for pattern making)
- Sketch pad
- Felt-tip markers
- Tape (washi tape or regular clear tape)
- Tracing paper

FOR PINNING + SEWING

- **Fabric:** Start a little stash of materials in colors you love in ½- to 2-yard (½- to 2-m) cuts. Aim for all-natural materials and fabrics that you will enjoy wearing.
- **Thread:** Try to go for 100 percent cotton thread, since we will be sewing with natural fibers. But really, any thread will do. Some cheaper threads can be hard to use, they might tangle or easily break, so try to buy the best quality you can.
- **Needles:** You can find packs of assorted hand-sewing needles, sometimes called "sharps," and they usually include different sizes and lengths. The hole is called the "eye." You will figure out which needles you like the most as you continue to sew. You will also notice that you might like using different needles for different types of fabrics. It is important to note that sharps are different from sewing machine needles.

- **Large pieces of paper:** You will use them to make your patterns. You can use wrapping paper, newspaper, or eventually invest in formal pattern paper.
- **Pins:** Inexpensive pins can snag your fabric or be challenging to use. Again, buy the best quality that you can. Pins come in different varieties. You might find that you like the all-metal ones best or the pins that have colorful glass heads. Some other options are quilting pins, which often have little shapes like butterflies, hearts, and flowers for the heads. They are super easy to use and a little more fun to look at.
- **Pincushion:** Store pins and needles in these little pillows. Pincushions are very easy to DIY.
- **Flexible tape measure:** So you can measure fabric and take body measurements easily.

FOR CUTTING

- **Paper scissors:** For cutting your pattern pieces
- **Fabric scissors:** For cutting your pattern out of fabric. Don't ever use these on paper; it will dull them.
- **Seam ripper:** To unpick any stitches

OTHER HELPFUL TOOLS

- **Fabric marker:** For stenciling and surface design
- **Notions:** This is a catchall term for objects used in a garment for decorative or functional purposes like buttons, snaps, elastic, and zippers.
- **Sewing machine:** All of the projects in this book can be sewn by hand, so a machine is optional. If you have a machine, we highly

suggest giving it a name! Like Emerald or Ethel (these are the names of Lesley's machines). We also recommend getting familiar with your sewing machine manual because it has everything that you need to know to operate your machine in a safe way. Go over it before you start to operate your machine, and keep it on your bookshelf, in your sewing space.

- **Journal:** This is the place where you will document your experience as you find your voice in fashion. Use it to take notes as explained on page 30—or even to keep a list of all the tools you'll need! Your journal is key.

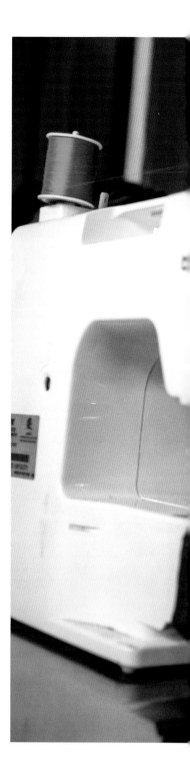

Hidden Figure of Fashion:

DONYALE LUNA

(1945–1979)

Donyale Luna was the world's first Black supermodel. Her face graced the cover of many fashion magazines, and she appeared in underground films of the 1960s and 1970s.

Born Peggy Ann Freeman in Detroit, Michigan, she was described as a shy and odd child. Her father worked at the Ford automotive plant and her mother was a secretary for a Christian organization. The home was not a happy place because her parents argued often. Donyale dreamed of escaping the torment of her household. After taking theater and acting classes in high school, at age eighteen she started calling herself Donyale George Luna.

Her modeling career began in the United States but did not fully take off until she moved to Europe. In December 1965, she arrived in London during the Youthquake movement and quickly became a part of the scene. Youthquake was a 1960s movement, for teens and by teens, that took away the dominance of European fashion houses. The term was coined by *Vogue* magazine's editor-in-chief Diana Vreeland.

Donyale was the first Black model to appear on the cover of any *Vogue* magazine, in British *Vogue* in March 1966. She wore a Chloé dress and stunning gold earrings by Italian designer Mimi di N. The editor of British *Vogue* at the time, Beatrix Miller, stated that she made the decision to put Donyale on the cover of the magazine because "She happens to be a marvelous shape—angular and immensely tall and strange. She has a kind of bite and personality." Later that year, *TIME* magazine called 1966 the Luna year. "She is a creature of contrasts," the magazine wrote.

The monumental *Vogue* cover made her an instant international celeb and one of the most sought-after models in the world. For the next decade, she was a regular in print and on the runway.

In 1976, she married Italian fashion photographer Luigi Cazzaniga, in California, and her daughter, Dream, was born in 1977. Dream's name was inspired by Dr. King's well-known speech "I Have a Dream."

Donyale Luna died unexpectedly in 1979 at only thirty-three years old.

The brave contributions Donyale made are astonishing and to be celebrated. She was able to dominate fashion during a time when the industry did not recognize Black models. Somehow largely forgotten, she was more than just a striking figure; she was a distinct personality who was able to shift the conversation.

▶ Did you know that in 1974, Beverly Ann Johnson was the first Black model to appear on the cover of American *Vogue*?

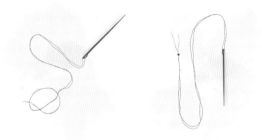

Threading the Needle

The first step in hand sewing is threading your needle. To thread your needle you will:

1. Cut some thread. The distance from the tip of your index finger to your elbow will work for this.
2. Thread your needle. Push the thread through the eye of the needle and draw it down until both ends of the thread meet.
3. Make a knot that is round and small at the end of the thread.

Stitching with Soul

The good news is that all of the projects in this book can be stitched by hand. Not everything can be sewn by machine anyway, so we wanted to zero in on hand sewing. (Though these projects could be sewn on a machine, too.) Hand sewing is is a great option because you can do it anywhere. Keep in mind: You are not a machine, so your stitches do not have to be perfect. Just like in life, imperfections can be beautiful! Let's see your *hand in your stitches*.

A BIT ABOUT KNOTS

Bad in hair (unless they are Bantu), good for thread.

With hand sewing, knots happen at the start and the end of your project. You will have to tie a knot when you thread your needle and another knot when you finish stitching or you run out of thread. Tie the knot close to the fabric or your stitches might pop. Knots should be hidden, so always finish stitching on the underside side of the fabric, which should also be the side you started on.

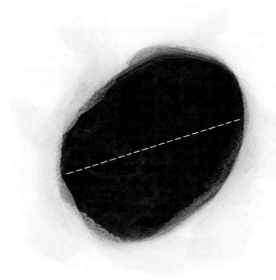

Stitches

The simple stitches you will need to know for this book are the running stitch, backstitch, overcast stitch, and topstitch.

RUNNING STITCH

The most popular, and the one that you might already know. This stitch is made by drawing the needle up from the underside of the fabric through to the topside of the fabric, then dipping it back into the topside a short distance away, over and over again with even spacing.

In addition to sewing two pieces of fabric together, this stitch can be used for topstitching, gathering, or basting.

BACKSTITCH

This stitch is a favorite because it is the strongest and the closest to a machine-sewn stitch. Draw the thread up through the fabric and make a long forward stitch along the seamline, then bring the needle a short stitch backward on the underside of the fabric, and bring it through to the topside. Take a long forward stitch again, going past the end of the first forward stitch about halfway, then bring the needle backward on the underside to the top of the first forward stitch. Repeat this, forming a line of stitches on both sides of the fabric. The ones on the underside are longer than the ones on the top side.

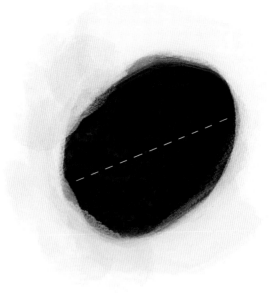

OVERCAST STITCH

This stitch is also called a whipstitch. It connects two pieces of fabric by using a series of loops along the side of the pieces. Anchor the thread at the end of the seamline, then draw the thread at a slight angle over the raw edge of the fabric and insert the needle again into the seamline from the underside, and repeat to the end. Don't draw the thread too tight; you want to keep the seam allowance flat. The distance between stitches will vary from project to project but it's always nice to have them close together. This stitch is easy to make and useful when finishing projects and sewing on patches.

TOPSTITCH

A topstitch is a looser running stitch that is used for decorative purpose or to help finish a project by securing its parts in place. You can also make this stitch by machine.

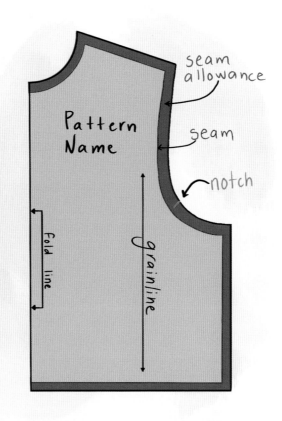

seam
allowance

seam

notch

Pattern
Name

Fold line

grainline

Working with Patterns

Pattern Markings: On each piece of a pattern you'll find various markings, including the pattern's name, the quantity you need to cut of each piece, the direction of the grainline, and the notches you'll need to mark using chalk, a pen, or cutout triangles.

Grainline: The grainline relates to the weave of the fabric, and it is found along the threads running lengthwise on the fabric.

Seam Allowance: The distance between the edge of the fabric and the seamline.

Seamline: The line you will sew on.

Fold line: If you see this marking on a pattern piece, the pattern must be placed on the fabric fold before cutting out so that it's cut in one large piece instead of two.

Notches: Notches are very small wedges cut into or marked along the seam allowance that help to match the corresponding seams during garment construction.

Working with Fabric

Here are some details about fabric you should know. You will want to make sure that you line everything up correctly so that your projects are sewn right. You will also want to sew on the grainline, meaning in the direction the threads are running. Fabric has three grains: straight, cross, and bias (45 degrees). We will only be sewing on the straight grain.

Selvage: An edge produced on woven fabric during manufacture that prevents it from unraveling. This usually has colors, shapes, or words woven into it. This part of the fabric may be slightly stiffer than the main fabric. This part of the fabric is not typically used unless you find it interesting and decide to include it in your design in a creative way.

Raw edge: The cut edge of the fabric.

Topside: Also called right side. The printed side of the fabric—usually the side you want to show when you finish the project. When sewing seams together, you usually do so with the right sides facing so that any ends end up on the wrong side.

Underside: Also called wrong side. The inside-facing side of the fabric that is not as vividly printed.

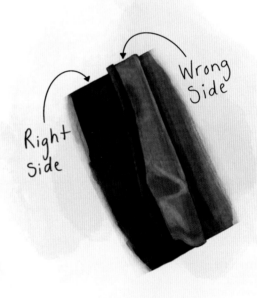

HOW TO SEW ON A BUTTON

1. Thread your needle (see page 48).

2. Starting on the wrong side of the fabric, underneath the button, poke the needle up through the first hole. Bring your needle down through the other hole and to the wrong side of the fabric. Repeat this for six to seven passes so it's very secure. If there are four holes in your button, repeat with the other pair of holes.

3. End with the needle on the wrong side of the fabric and make a tight knot to hold everything in place.

WEAR A CROWN

Wearing a headpiece has always been a hallmark of Black style and is rooted in tradition, dating back to enslaved Africans in the 1600s, 1700s, and 1800s. This trend continued and was picked up in a new way in the 1920s during the Harlem Renaissance, when wearing a beautiful hat was a sign of economic success and status for women. Over the years, dress hats have become an art form, and you will often see many elders of the Black church wearing neatly decorated, beautifully made hats on Sunday mornings. These embellished headpieces serve as a symbol of pride and as a reminder that we are Queens.

#Crownyourself and flaunt your Black Girl Magic by wearing a headpiece when you need added sparkle!

Materials

- 1 yard (1 m) decorative lace crochet trim at least 4 inches (10 cm) wide
- Parchment paper or a trash bag
- Spray starch
- Gold acrylic paint
- Paintbrush
- Gold glitter
- 1 yard (1 m) thin rope, rickrack, or other trim, such as lace
- Hot-glue gun and glue
- Two small side combs or bobby pins (optional)
- Jewel, ribbon, tulle, flower, feather, or bead embellishments
- Basic sewing supplies—needle, fabric scissors, thread, pins

Instructions

1. Wrap the lace trim around your head where you would like the crown to sit, taking into account how you style your hair. Carefully place a pin to mark the length. Cut the trim ½ inch (12 mm) beyond the pin.

2. Cover your work surface with parchment paper or a trash bag, place the lace on top, and spray with starch on both sides until it is soaked.

let dry 12h

3. Let the lace sit overnight so that it dries completely. You want it to be hard enough that it can stand on its own when you turn it into a crown.

4. After the starch is dry, paint one side of the lace gold. Add gold glitter while the paint is still wet for an extra bit of sparkle. Glitter can spread all over the place, so you may want to do this step outside, if the weather permits. Let it dry, then paint the other side.

↻ paint on other side

5. Once the paint is dry on the lace, place your additional trim (thin rope/rickrack) along the front bottom of the lace (the side with glitter should face out) using your hot-glue gun. Make sure you have a stand or cardboard scrap to sit your glue gun on when you are not using it so you don't get glue on your table.

6. Next, you will join both ends of the lace to make the crown. Overlap the ends by about ½ inch (12 mm); you can place a drop of hot glue to hold it in place. With your needle and thread, sew a neat running stitch (see page 49) to further secure it together.

7. If you decide to sew in combs to the inside bottom of the crown, one on either side, use the overcast stitch (see page 50). Combs will prevent your crown from flying off in the wind; another option is to just use two bobby pins to secure the crown in place.

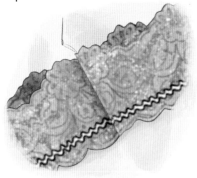

8. Embellish and finish it! Add gemstones, a tiny ribbon bow, small flowers, feathers, or beading to your crown. When possible, sew them on, but you may find that it is easier to use glue. Make sure the items are lightweight so your crown will not become too heavy and start to droop.

Look into the mirror. What do you see? How does this crown celebrate your hair?

Review the reflection questions on page 30 and take notes in your fashion journal.

▶ At the 2021 presidential inauguration for Joe Biden, we saw poet Amanda Gorman wear a fiery red headband that resembled a crown to recite her poem "The Hill We Climb."

DENIM SCRUNCHIE

Unleash your inner eighties girl! Back in the day, we loved rocking a high ponytail, to the side, with a colorful scrunchie. Make your own set of scrunchies to hold your hair in place—they're much more fun than plain old rubber bands. Grab some denim and elastic, and let's sew an accessory that is stylish and practical.

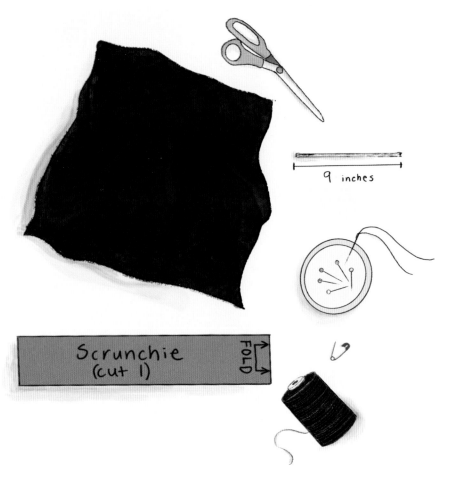

9 inches

Scrunchie (cut 1)

FOLD

Materials

- Piece of denim (the lighter the weight the better)
- Safety pin
- ¼ inch (6 mm) elastic, 9 inches (23 cm) long
- Basic sewing supplies—needle, fabric scissors, thread, pins
- Sewing machine with sewing thread to match your fabric (optional)

Instructions

1. Cut the denim into a rectangle measuring 3½ inches × 22 inches (9 cm × 56 cm).

2. Fold the rectangle in half lengthways with the right sides facing. Using a running stitch (see page 49), sew ¼ inch (6 mm) away from the long raw edge to form a tube, leaving both short ends unsewn (or use your sewing machine).

5. Turn the raw edges of the tube to the inside and hand-stitch all the way around the folded edges with an overcast stitch (see page 50), to close your scrunchie!

3. Turn the tube right side out. You may need to use a pencil or paintbrush to help push the fabric through.

4. Attach a safety pin to the end of the elastic and insert the elastic through the tube. Tie the elastic ends together in a tight knot. The fabric tube should naturally gather (scrunch) around the elastic.

Scrunchies are cool because they make not-so-great hair days okay. And you can wear them all sorts of ways—scrunchies look fab with box braids, pigtails, or natural hair!

ANKARA TRIANGLE REVERSIBLE HEADWRAP

Wearing a headwrap is a style to love. It is a way to experiment with color and bring a bit of interest to your outfits. Some headwraps can be expensive to buy, but you can make your own reversible head wrap in about an hour. Selecting your Ankara fabric is the fun part of this project. Since this wrap is double-sided it can be worn two different ways. Let's make it!

Materials

- 1 yard (1 m) each of 2 different cotton fabrics (2 yards/2 m total)
- Basic sewing supplies—needle, fabric scissors, thread, pins
- Sewing machine with sewing thread to match your fabric (optional)

Instructions

1. Cut two pieces of fabric into a triangle using these measurements: 38 inches × 24 inches × 24 inches. For your reversible triangle wrap to be functional, each piece of fabric needs to be the same size.

2. Match the two pieces of fabric with right sides together. Make sure everything is neat and flat. If you want, you can iron the fabric. Pin the pieces together. Using backstitch (see page 49), sew ¼ inch (6 mm), away from the edge all the way around, leaving about 5 inches (13 cm) open on one side, or use your sewing machine and leave ⅝ inch (1.5 cm) seam allowance.

3. Flip the reversible triangle wrap right side out through the hole you left on the side. Tuck the edges of the opening neatly to the inside, pin them in place, and sew the hole shut using an overcast stitch (see page 50).

4. Clip any excess threads. Press the wrap flat.

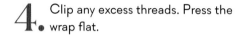

Headwraps have a lavish, long, and complicated history because they were one of the few cultural pieces enslaved Africans were able to bring to the Americas during the transatlantic slave trade period. Wearing a wrap was considered a symbol of social status, marital status, and family lineage in pre-colonial sub-Saharan Africa.

After you make your first headwrap, make it again in block print or bleach dye fabrics, or make your own Ankara-inspired print with fabric markers. What is the new meaning you're giving to the headwrap you will wear today?

▶ Ankara, commonly known as "Ankara print," "African print," or "African (Dutch) wax print," is a cotton fabric with bright colors and vibrant, tribal-like patterns and motifs.

PATRICK KELLY

(1954–1990)

Patrick Kelly was an adored fashion designer known as the "King of Cling" for his slinky, body-conscious dresses. Kelly's designs were celebrated for their over-the-top playful style, pop culture references, and nod to Black folklore. Of his many accomplishments, he was the first American to be inducted into the Chambre Syndicale, the illustrious governing body of the French ready-to-wear industry.

Kelly was born in Vicksburg, Mississippi, and was rasied by his mother, a home economics teacher, and his grandmother, a cook and a maid. Kelly's mother supported his interest in learning to sew and taught him to draw. His grandmother helped build his love of style by bringing home fashion magazines she got from the wealthy white family she worked for. After Kelly graduated from high school, he attended Jackson State University, where he studied art and African American history. But after two years he decided to move to Atlanta, Georgia, to pursue his passion for fashion.

While in Atlanta he worked at a thrift shop, giving him unlimited access to designer items including outerwear and dresses that were no longer neeed. He would upcycle the donated items, and he later sold them in a shop he opened. In 1979, he met supermodel Pat Cleveland, who suggested that Kelly study at the Parsons School of Design in New York. While at Parsons, Kelly was frustrated by a lack of support, and after a year in New York, he took Pat's advice *again* and moved to Paris, another fashion capital.

In 1985, his first commercial collection was featured in a six-page spread in *Elle France* magazine. This exposure led to a major investment in his business from a notable fashion company. This collaboration sent Kelly's designs soaring, and they were sold worldwide.

Kelly collected Black memorabilia and was known for including sometimes offensive or demeaning imagery in his designs. Dr. Monica L. Miller, professor of Africana Studies at Barnard, says that one of the ways he attempted to destigmatize racist memorabilia was by reusing, repurposing, and reappropriating it.

Kelly believed that women of all types should feel good about themselves. In 1987, he told *People* magazine, "I design for fat women, skinny women, all kinds of women. My message is, you're beautiful just the way you are." For example, at his show later that year, he featured a model who was eight months pregnant. This was replicated in 2018, by Rihanna for Savage × Fenty, with model Slick Woods, and again by Christian Siriano in 2020 at his socially distanced runway show.

Patrick Kelly's seemingly magical career ended abruptly, at age thirty-five, due to complications related to AIDS.

Kelly was an icon who usually wore oversized overalls and a biker's cap that said *Paris*. His favorite things were fried chicken, foie gras, and pearls. Kelly is remembered as a designer who directly addressed race in his work. One of his most famous quotes: "I design differently because I am Patrick Kelly, and Patrick Kelly is Black."

Kelly's use of playful buttons was inspired by his grandmother, who used mismatched buttons to mend her family's clothing. Add a mix of buttons to your sweatshirt as a nod to Patrick Kelly.

SCRAP EARRINGS

Earrings are divine. They dangle and drop, feel magical, and are surprisingly meaningful. In ancient African history, earrings stood for prosperity and protection; they also had ritualist and religious meanings. It is easy to create your own timeless treasures that you won't see anyone else wearing.

Materials

- Pattern (page 172)
- Fabric scraps
- Fabric scissors
- Paper
- Paper scissors
- Newspaper, old tablecloth, or trash bag
- Fabric glue (or Mod Podge)
- Small hole punch or a large needle
- Needle-nose pliers or tweezers
- Jump rings*
- Earring hooks*

*You can use inexpensive earrings from the beauty supply store that you take apart, to avoid having to buy all of the hardware separately.

Tip: make two pairs at a time—one for you and another for a friend.

Instructions

1. Place your pattern on top of a piece of fabric and pin the pattern to the fabric all the way around. Cut out the piece. Repeat for three more pieces of fabric and two pieces of paper.

2. Cover your work surface with newspaper, a tablecloth, or a trash bag. Carefully apply glue evenly to the front of the paper pieces and to the wrong side of two matching fabric pieces. Press the fabric pieces to the paper pieces, glued sides together. Apply glue to the back of the paper pieces and to the wrong side of the other two fabric pieces. Press the glued sides of the paper and fabric pieces together.

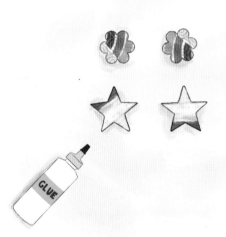

3. Let dry, then punch a hole through the fabric and paper stack at the top (about the same distance as shown in the illustration below) using a tiny hole punch or large needle.

4. With small pliers or tweezers, add jump rings to both earrings through the hole. Make sure you tightly close the loop so your earring won't fall off.

5. With small pliers or tweezers add earring hooks.

After you make a few pairs, what can you do next? Can you add topstitching (see page 50) or design your own textile? A half-and-half design with two different fabrics, or two different colors? Throw on another jump ring to have two tiers? Make sure your earrings stay lightweight so you take care of your earlobes.

REUSABLE FACE MASK

- -

Mask up if you feel icky. Wearing a reusable face mask is a way
to stop the spread of germs to yourself and others. That's one of
the many lessons we learned in 2020. Design your own line of
reusable masks that keep you fierce and protected. Use a fabric
print you adore or create your textile using one of the surface design
techniques on pages 141–148.

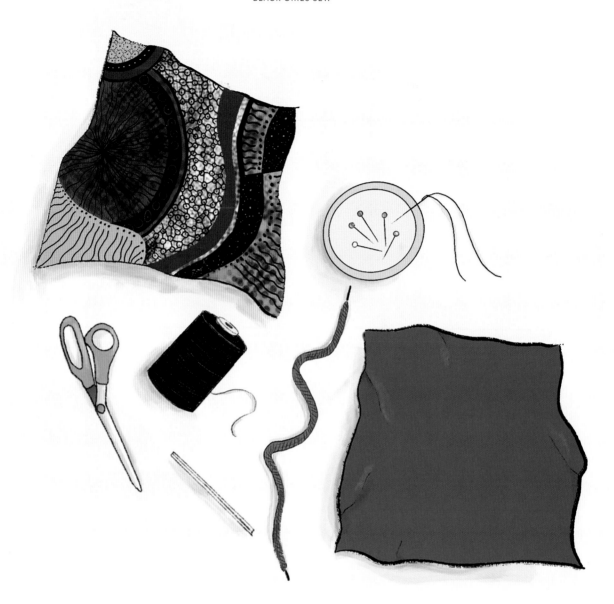

Materials

- Pattern (page 173)
- Two 7-inch × 7-inch (18 cm × 18 cm) squares of cotton fabric (one for the outside and one for the lining)
- Chalk
- Two shoestrings (you will need to cut them in half, creating four equal parts, each about 16 inches/40.5 cm long)

- Loop turner (optional)
- Nose wire, twist tie, or pipe cleaner (optional)
- Basic sewing supplies—needle, fabric scissors, thread, pins
- Sewing machine (optional)
- Iron (optional)

Instructions

1. Place your pattern on top of a piece of fabric near one corner and pin the pattern to the fabric all the way around. Cut out the piece. Mark the notches on the fabric using chalk or by cutting out little clips.

Repeat with the same fabric piece, then cut two additional pieces out of the other piece of fabric. You will cut four pieces total—two halves for the outer fabric and two halves for the lining.

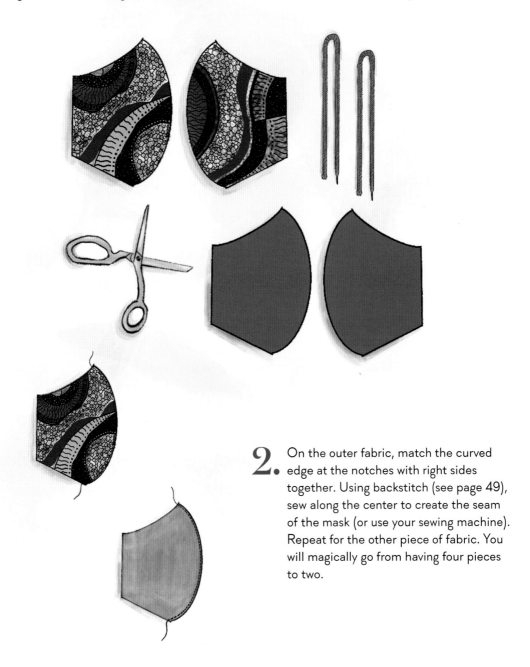

2. On the outer fabric, match the curved edge at the notches with right sides together. Using backstitch (see page 49), sew along the center to create the seam of the mask (or use your sewing machine). Repeat for the other piece of fabric. You will magically go from having four pieces to two.

77

3. Place your lining piece down with the right side up. Place the cut ends of the shoestrings on the mask corners so that they peek out just a bit, but the strings extend toward the center of the mask.

5. Pin through the shoestrings and layers to hold them in place. Using backstitch (see page 49), sew ¼ inch (6 mm) away from the edge all the way around the mask, leaving about 1¼ inches (3 cm) open on one long side (or use your sewing machine).

4. Place the outer fabric on top with the right side down—pretend you are making a sandwich. You should now have both layers of your mask stacked on each other with right sides together, and four shoestrings sandwiched between them.

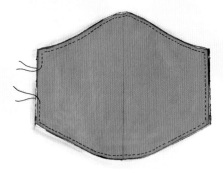

Tip: Be careful not to catch any of the shoestrings in the seam except on the edges where you want to secure them.

6. Your mask is wrong side out now, so turn it right side out through the hole you left open. If you have a loop turner, it comes in handy now. Tuck the edges of the opening neatly to the inside and pin them in place to close up the hole.

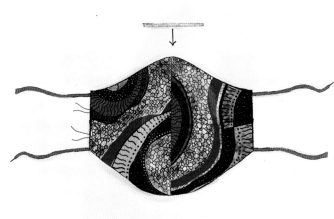

7. Top stitch around the edge of the mask (see page 50). Topstitching will give the mask some extra stability, secure the shoestrings, keep the lining from rolling forward, and close up the hole.

Tip: Before you close the opening you may want to slide in a sandwich tie or pipe cleaner to create a nose wire that keeps the mask fitting close around your nose. The top stitch that you do in step 7 will keep the nose wire in place.

You may also want to add a pleat between the ties after you topstitch to get a better fit around your face. A pleat is a simple fold in fabric that is held in place by a stitch.

When you finish making your mask, you can press it with an iron. This step has no functional value, but it does make the mask look better. If you're not too bothered about that, feel free to skip ironing!

That's it! You're done! Remake it—and this time add embellishments like patches, beading, or an applique, or color it with a fabric marker; be sure to check out the Embellishment section on page 141 for more ideas. Make a bunch so you can share or sell. #Maskup

► Fabric Facts: The goal of a mask is to stop droplets from spreading. So you want to go for something that filters germs out while still being able to breathe easily. We suggest 100 percent woven cotton like Ankara. You can use an inexpensive but breathable fabric like muslin as the lining.

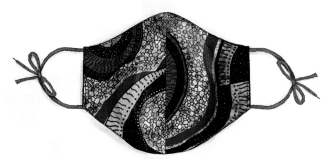

NO-WASTE WAIST BAG

Belt bags are an eighties throwback trend that will likely be here forever. Grab your fabric and sewing supplies and get started. In about an hour you'll have a chic fashion statement around your waist, without any waste.

Pair it with your eighties scrunchie—you could use the same fabric and have a matching set!

Materials

- 1 yard (1 m) lightweight cotton fabric
- Basic sewing supplies—needle, fabric scissors, thread, pins
- Sewing machine with sewing thread to match your fabric (optional)
- Iron

Instructions

1. Cut the fabric into two 9-inch × 26-inch (23 cm × 66 cm) rectangles for the body of the bag.

2. Stack the two pieces together with wrong sides facing. Using backstitch (see page 49), sew ¼ inch (6 mm) away from the edge along three sides of the rectangle, leaving one of the shorter sides unsewn (or use your sewing machine). Along the unsewn edge, fold the seam allowances down to the wrong side ⅝ inch (16 mm) to make a hem. Using backstitch, sew the hem in place.

9 inches

26 inches

3. Flip the piece right side out so that all the seam allowances are hidden inside.

5. Create a fold 6 inches (15 cm) from the top and iron down the fold.

4. Create a fold line at 8 inches (20 cm) down from the end of the bag with the opening and sew along the right and left sides of the rectangle to hold it in place.

6. Using topstitch (see page 50), sew a seam 1¼ inches (3 cm) from the fold to create a space for your belt.

7. Cut a 1-yard-long × 4-inch-wide (1 m × 10 cm) strip of matching or complementary fabric on the fabric's bias, then make it into a double-fold bias tape as instructed below. You may need help with this part since the steam from the iron can be quite hot. This piece becomes the belt. Here's how to do it:

- Fold the strip in half lengthwise with the wrong sides together. Press.
- Open the strip again, then fold one raw edge of the strip to the center crease and press. Repeat on the other side. Fold in half again, on the center crease. Press. You should now have a 1-inch-wide (2.5 cm) double bias tape.

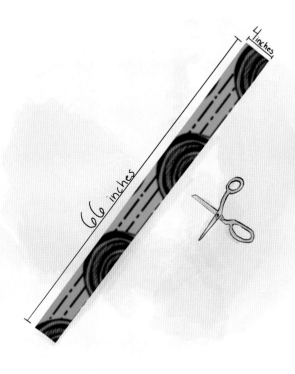

8. Pin the bias tape along the open edge. The raw fabric edges should be sandwiched between each side of the bias tape.

9. Using topstitch (see page 50), sew along the open edge of the bias tape. Thread the bias tape through the opening at the top of the bag. Your belt is complete!

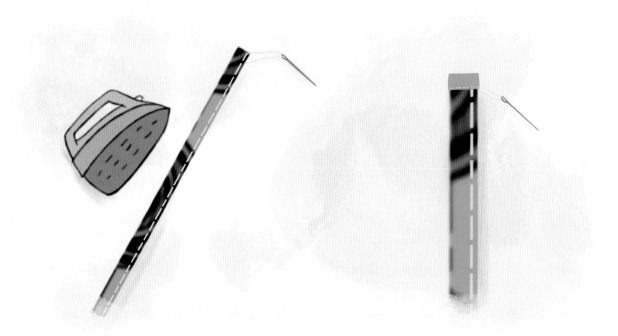

Now that you've strapped on your first bag, let's try it again! Experiment with the size and material or add a pocket, similar to the Tote Bag (see page 91).

Hidden Figure of Fashion:

ELIZABETH HOBBS KECKLEY

(1818–1907)

Known for her sewing skills, networking savvy, and beauty, Elizabeth Hobbs Keckley was a former slave turned sole business owner, saleswoman, and designer. Washington, D.C., socialites hired her as their dressmaker because of her sophisticated style. She was best known for her work as personal dressmaker and confidante of First Lady Mary Todd Lincoln.

Born in Dinwiddie, Virginia, she was the only child of her mother Agnes, who made clothing for the family that owned her and other slaves. When Hobbs Keckley was four, she became a nursemaid that tended to infants. As she grew, she was able to help her mother make clothing. At times she was subject to harsh treatment, but when her talents as a seamstress started to show, her life began to change and get slightly better. Hobbs Keckley and her mother were eventually sold to another family that moved to St. Louis, Missouri.

Even with this new family, times were hard, but from her work as a seamstress, she was eventually able to buy her and her son George's freedom from her St. Louis owners for $1,200 in 1855. (That would be the equivalent of $37,000 today.)

At the age of forty, she moved to D.C., where she started off working as a seamstress for a dressmaker. She made only $2.50 a day but was able to save and eventually establish her own dressmaking business. Remember, these were the days when you could not just pop into a department store to get a dress—everything was made for you, whether by a family member or a dressmaker. Fashion at this time typically copied French trends; whatever was happening at the French court was what D.C. women wanted to wear. According to the Smithsonian Institution, Hobbs Keckley "was known to be *the* dressmaker in D.C. because her garments had an extraordinary fit." Her design style utilized clean lines and was without a lot of lace, ribbon, flounces, or frills, a simplified version of sophisticated Victorian fashion.

Hobbs Keckley quickly amassed a client base and was sought out by many politicians' wives. Through this connection, she met First Lady Mary Todd Lincoln. Mary Todd had a reputation for wearing floral prints and bright colors, but when Elizabeth started dressing her, her look became tasteful and more refined. Elizabeth and Mary became good friends. In 1862, the same year that slaves were emancipated in D.C., Elizabeth helped Mary after her son Willie Lincoln passed and later after the president's assassination. Elizabeth's son, George, had died in 1861 while serving in the Union army. She could empathize with the First Lady's grief.

In 1868, she wrote her memoir, *Behind the Scenes, or Thirty Years a Slave and Four Years in the White House.* At age seventy-four, in 1892, Hobbs Keckley was offered a position at Wilberforce University in Ohio as the head

of the Department of Sewing and Domestic Science Arts. After her tenure at Wilberforce she moved back to D.C. into the National Home for Destitute Colored Women and Children. This was where she lived until she died in May 1907.

Sewing talent took Elizabeth Hobbs Keckley from being enslaved to owning a thriving business as a Black woman during the 1800s. She understood the importance of making contacts, a skill that allowed her to network and meet the right people. Elizabeth pressed forward even when times were hard. There is so much to take note of in Elizabeth Hobbs Keckley's story.

BLACK GIRLS SEW TOTE

Are you ready to sew the perfect tote? This bag is ideal for carrying most things—it even has a small pocket in the front so you can quickly grab what you need—and it's simple to make. You can wash and carry this bag over and over again. Make yours from a variety of woven fabrics; we chose denim for its strength, resilience, and versatility. Show your pride and connection to Black Girls Sew!

Materials

- ¼ yard (23 cm) white canvas or duck cloth
- Ruler
- Masking or washi tape
- Pencil
- 1- to 1½-inch (2.5- to 4-cm) alphabet stencils
- Black fabric marker
- 1 yard (1 m) denim
- Iron
- 1½ yards (1.5 m) nylon or cotton strapping (in black or your favorite color)
- Chalk
- Basic sewing supplies—needle, fabric scissors, thread, pins
- Sewing machine with sewing thread to match your fabric (optional)

Instructions

MAKING & STENCILING THE POCKET

1. Cut an 8-inch × 8-inch (20 cm × 20 cm) square from the white canvas.

2. Fold ½ inch (1.3 cm) to the wrong side around all four sides of your square and press flat. The square should now measure about 7 inches × 7 inches (18 cm × 18 cm).

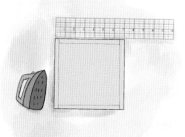

3. Using backstitch (see page 49), sew ¼ inch (6 mm) away from the edge around all four sides of the pocket to keep the sides flat (or use your sewing machine).

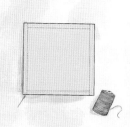

4. Use your ruler to mark 1 inch (2.5 cm) from the side to your left. Place a piece of tape vertically. This will be where you start each line of your stenciling.

5. Use your ruler to measure 2 inches (5 cm) down from the square's top edge and mark a line perpendicular to the first line across the square with tape. Mark two more lines spaced 2 inches (5 cm) apart below the first line. You are making a grid, with three spaces in total, for your stencil. This will help keep your stencil straight.

6. With your pencil, use your stencils to draw the words BLACK GIRLS SEW—one word on each line.

7. After you have penciled the words in, use your black fabric marker to color in each letter. Remove the tape and set the pocket aside until it is time to place it on the tote.

MAKING THE BAG

1. Cut a rectangle of denim that is 15 inches × 30 inches (38 cm × 76 cm).

2. On the short ends of the rectangle, fold the edges 1 inch (2.5 cm) toward the wrong side of the fabric, press, and pin. Using backstitch (see page 49), sew across 1¼ inches (3 cm) away from the folded edge on each end.

3. With the right side facing up, measure 4 inches (10 cm) down from one hem and 4 inches (10 cm) in from each side and mark with chalk. Center the finished pocket, right side facing up, in this area. Make sure the top of the pocket is pointing toward the hem. Pin the two sides and bottom of the pocket to the rectangle.

4. If you have a machine, you may want to use a zigzag stitch to sew around the three sides of the pocket. You will want to pivot around the two bottom corners by making sure your needle is in the fabric when you lift the presser foot and turn the fabric to the desired angle or direction. Make sure you reverse stitch when you start and stop to reinforce the pocket's top corners. If you are not using a machine, your pocket is fine as is!

94

5. Cut the nylon or cotton strapping to make two straps that are 20 to 23 inches (51 to 58 cm) long, depending on your height—the taller you are, the longer you may want your straps.

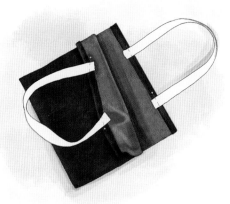

6. Flip the rectangle over so the wrong side is facing up. Measure 4 inches (10 cm) in from the hem edge and one side edge and mark with chalk. Fold the strap's cut end under, about ½ to 1 inch (1.3 to 2.5 cm), and pin the strap to the wrong side of the rectangle at the mark. Using backstitch (see page 49), sew a rectangle around the base of the strap, stitching close to the edges on the three open sides, then sew two diagonal lines to make an × inside the rectangle, to reinforce it (or use your sewing machine). Repeat on the opposite end of the same side with the other end of the same strap. Repeat on the other side of the rectangle with the other strap.

7. Fold the rectangle in half with right sides together. Using backstitch, sew ⅝ inch (1.5 cm) away from the side edges (or use your sewing machine). If you use a sewing machine, remember to reverse stitch when you start and stop to reinforce the sides so your bag will stay strong.

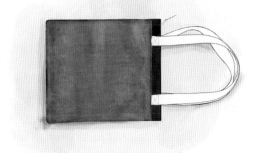

8. Clean up any stray threads. Turn the bag right side out. Congrats—you're done!

You are #official now that you've made a Black Girls Sew tote! How would you remake this bag? You can use an array of different approaches to size, embellishments, and materials.

TULLE TUTU

Wearing a tulle tutu is a way to add joy to any outfit. This tutu requires only a tiny bit of sewing. Tutus are amazing because they give you the silhouette of a ballerina, adding an air of magic wherever you go. Wear this tutu under a dress to a party for a puffy, fun silhouette. Or wear it for cosplay—maybe you want to reenact your favorite fairy tale. Or maybe just wear it over leggings to dance around while listening to your fashion playlist.

Materials

- Tape measure
- 1 to 1½ yards (1 to 1.5 m) ½-inch (1.3 cm) elastic
- 5 yards (5 m) tulle
- Basic sewing supplies—needle, fabric scissors, thread, pins

Instructions

1. To figure out the correct length of elastic, measure your waist with your tape measure. Make sure the tape measure is snug, but not tight. Write down the length. Subtract 3 inches (7.5 cm) from your waist measurement and cut your elastic to this length. For example, if your waist is 30 inches (76 cm), subtract 3 (7.5): You will cut a 27-inch (69 cm) piece of elastic.

2. Bring the ends of the elastic together (without twisting), then overlap the ends by 1 inch (2.5 cm). Pin together. Using a very tight running stitch (see page 49), sew the ends together in the overlap to make an elastic loop.

3. Cut the entire piece of tulle into 4-inch (10 cm) wide strips. Do not worry about cutting them to a perfect width, but aim for about 4 inches (10 cm) for each. Each strip will be approximately 64 inches (163 cm) long.

Fold each strip of tulle in half lengthwise. Fold again, so the strip is in quarters. Fold this once more in half widthwise.

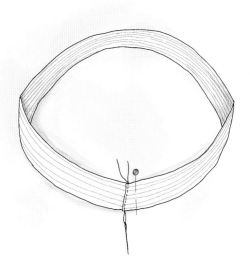

4. Step into the elastic ring and pull it up around your upper thighs. Or you can get a friend to wear the elastic ring to make adding the tulle to the elastic easier. Bring the middle of the tulle strip under the elastic so that the loop extends above the elastic. Take the two ends and pull them up and through the loop and back down. Pull it snug.

5. Repeat for all the tulle strips, working your way around the elastic. Fluff out the tulle as you go. Before you know it: *ta-da*! Tutu complete!

You can make tutus in lots of colors to create photo-ready looks! Wear it with your crown! Think Misty Copeland's life-in-motion vibes.

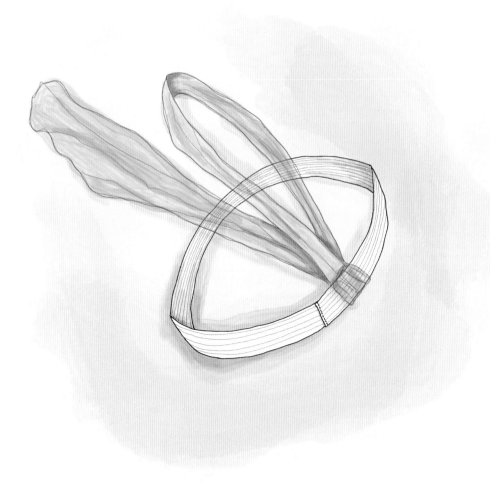

FASHION CAPITAL SWEATSHIRT

New York, Paris, London, and Milan are the biggest fashion capitals in the world. There's also Lagos, Tokyo, Berlin, Beijing, and Barcelona. Fashion capitals are cities that have an influence on global fashion trends. These cities usually design, manufacture, and sell lots of garments. They also hold the major runway shows during the spring and fall seasons.

What is your favorite fashion-forward city? Do a little research. Find out who the Black fashion designers are that capture your attention, and where they live or work. Some of our favorites include Kerby Jean-Raymond or Tracy Reese from New York; Olivier Rousteing from Paris; Stella Jean from Milan; Lanre da Silva from Lagos; Buki Akomolafe from Berlin; and Ozwald Boateng from London.

Then create this upcycled sweatshirt with a place you'd love to explore (or visit again). Tap into your inner jet-setter.

Materials

- Applique letter templates (page 171)
- Pencil
- Tracing paper
- 100% cotton fabric scraps
- Pen or pencil
- Paper scissors
- Iron
- Buttons

- Fusible bonding tape (Stitch Witchery or Dritz Bonding Web)
- Plain old or thrifted sweatshirt
- Basic sewing supplies—needle, fabric scissors, thread, pins
- Sewing machine with sewing thread to match your fabric (optional)

Instructions

1. Select the city for your applique. Using the template on page 171, trace the letters onto the tracing paper. (Or, if you want to pick a different city, choose your own typeface—make sure it's big and bold!—print out the letters and then trace.) Cut out each letter to make the letter pattern pieces.

2. Pin your pattern pieces to the scraps of fabric and cut each letter out. Feel free to mix it up with prints that represent your style or go with a single solid fabric.

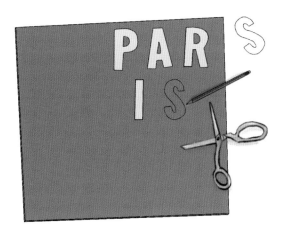

3. Fold your sweatshirt in half to find the center of the front, mark it, and evenly place the letters on each side of the center. They look good on a curve. Play around with the placement of the letters. Make sure you like the layout before moving forward.

4. Place the fusible bonding material on the back of the fabric letters, trimming it so none of the fusible bonding material peeks around the edges of the letters, or you may get the glue on your iron. Follow the instructions on the package to fuse each letter onto your sweatshirt. Make sure everything is smooth and flat on the sweatshirt.

5. Topstitch (page 50) neatly around each letter, by hand or with your machine. If you are doing this by machine you could topstitch with a zigzag stitch.

6. Add more applique patches in whatever shapes you want to give the shirt an extra element of interest. Go for texture, prints, and bits that tell the story of the fashion capital you are exploring. And check out page 53 for how to sew on buttons for even more added flare.

Now wear your sweatshirt with pride and share some of the info you learned while researching your city! This project is simple to replicate. Create a second sweatshirt with another fashion capital or try a word or phrase like INSPIRE, or GOOD VIBES ONLY, or SEW FLY!

Hidden Figure of Fashion:

ZELDA WYNN VALDES

(1905–2001)

Zelda Wynn Valdes was a fashion designer and the first Black business owner on (the iconic) Broadway in New York City. Her client list included several stars from the forties to the eighties, like Dorothy Dandridge, Josephine Baker, Gladys Knight, and opera legend Jessye Norman.

Zelda Christian Barbour was born in Chambersburg, Pennsylvania, and was the eldest of seven children. Her interest in learning to sew came from watching her grandmother's seamstress. Her first attempt at design was when she offered to create a dress for her grandmother. "She said, 'Daughter, you can't sew for me. I'm too tall and too big,'" Zelda recalled in a 1994 interview with the *New York Times*, but the dress she created was a perfect fit.

She was trained as a classical pianist at the Catholic Conservatory of Music and after graduating from Chambersburg High School in 1923, her immediate family moved to White Plains, New York, where she started to work in the tailoring shop her uncle owned and in the stockroom at a high-end boutique. The combination of these experiences helped her to climb the ladder, eventually finding herself as the shop's first Black sales clerk and tailor.

Being a Black woman and a seamstress was a stress-filled, underappreciated job at the time.

Zelda was basically a low-wage service worker, which made it difficult to break into the world of high-fashion custom design.

After more than a decade of professional tailoring experience, she opened her boutique on Broadway and West 158th Street in 1948, making it one of the first Black-owned businesses on Broadway. After a couple of years, she bravely moved Chez Zelda to 151 West 57th Street in Midtown. Here, she had a staff of Black dressmakers and charged about $1,000 per gown; this would be equivalent to almost $10,000 today.

The relocation was a success, and Zelda began to work with a slew of stars, including Dorothy Dandridge, Josephine Baker, Ruby Dee, Eartha Kitt, Ella Fitzgerald, and Mae West, just to name a few.

Designers always have that one thing that makes them unique—Zelda had the ability to turn satin, silk organza, and knit jersey into desirable, wearable art. She was known as a designer who could fit a dress to any size, sometimes by just looking at the client. "I only fit her once in twelve years," she told the *New York Times* of her longtime client Ella Fitzgerald. "I had to do everything by imagination for her."

Zelda was flexible and practical in her creativity. Her clientele included Black women who were not famous but could afford her designs. Having a dazzling roster of superstar clients was certainly a selling point.

Constance C. R. White, author of *How to Slay: Inspiration from the Queens and Kings of Black Style* and former executive fashion director at *Elle* magazine and *Essence* says,

"Zelda was operating in a time when Parisian fashion was really ascendant, so it's pretty remarkable what she was able to accomplish." She goes on, "She definitely helped to popularize and define the look of a woman's curvy silhouette, but it was always elegant. The femininity that Zelda promulgated into her designs was very powerful."

A year after opening her store, Zelda helped found and was named president of the New York chapter of the National Association of Fashion and Accessory Designers. This was a coalition and support group for Black designers working in an industry that frequently sought to exclude them.

Zelda was all about paying it forward. She created a program in Harlem that taught thousands of children to sew. Through her teaching, she met Arthur Mitchell, the first Black principal dancer

of the New York City Ballet and founder of the Dance Theatre of Harlem. In 1970, Mitchell recruited Zelda, then sixty-five years old, to design the costumes for his company.

In 1989, Chez Zelda, still located in midtown Manhattan, would close, but Zelda continued to design for the Dance Theatre of Harlem until she died in September 2001. She was ninety-seven years old.

Zelda Wynn Valdes was not considered a "fashion designer" in the way we see designers celebrated today, with massive Instagram followings and appearances on the red carpet with their clients, but she should have the spotlight now. During her long and colorful career, Zelda had lots of firsts while redefining fashion one stitch at a time.

▶ Zelda was also responsible for creating the first Playboy Bunny costume.

VINTAGE-INSPIRED WRAP TOP

This top is inspired by a decade in fashion: the fifties! The look for teens during this time was fitted and short tops with loose wide skirts and cinched-high waists. Popular Black designers of this decade were Ann Lowe, Zelda Wynn Valdes, and Arthur McGee. The 1950s presented many challenges—the Civil Rights Movement had begun and Black people in America, especially teens, rallied for changes socially, legally, and politically to stop discrimination and end segregation. Reimagine the 1950s and consider its style, then create this top. Ask a family member who was alive in the 1950s what life was like. Bring inspiration from the conversation into your design concept.

Note: This top fits like a small or X-small. For a larger size, increase the dimensions of the fabric you cut for the desired fit.

Materials

- 1 yard (1 m) woven fabric like cotton, Ankara, voile, or muslin
- Loop turner or safety pin
- Chalk
- A bowl or something large and round to trace (The diameter should be between 6–7.5 inches/15–19 cm.)

- 1 yard (1 m) bias tape (We suggest the widest you can find.)
- Iron
- Basic sewing supplies—needle, fabric scissors, thread, pins
- Sewing machine

Instructions

1. Cut three rectangles out of your fabric to the following dimensions:
2 inches × 42 inches (5 cm × 1 m)
5 inches × 42 inches (13 cm × 1 m)
27 inches × 42 inches (69 cm × 1 m)

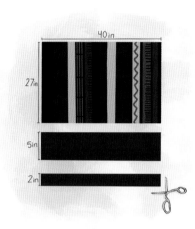

3. On the wider strip, sew each end closed on a diagonal, as pictured in the illustration. Carefully clip the excess fabric off the corners.

2. Fold the 2-inch (5 cm) wide rectangle in half lengthwise, right sides together, to make a 1-inch (2.5 cm) wide strip. Using backstitch (see page 49), sew ⅛ inch (3 mm) from the raw edge (or use your sewing machine, leaving a ⅝-inch [1.5 cm] allowance). Repeat with the 5-inch (13 cm) wide rectangle to make a 2½-inch (6.5 cm) wide strip.

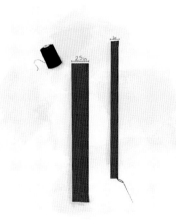

4. Cut both sewn rectangle strips in half so you have four pieces. Turn each piece right side out. You may want to use a loop turner to make it easier to turn. Press flat with an iron. These are the sashes you will wrap around your waist.

5. Take the 27-inch (69 cm) wide rectangle and fold each edge ½ inch (1.3 cm) toward the wrong side. Fold over another ½ inch (1.3 cm) so the raw edge is hidden. Using backstitch (see page 49), sew just under ½ inch (12 mm) away from the edge on all four sides (or use your sewing machine). This is called a double hem.

6. Fold the hemmed rectangle in half widthwise with right sides together and place it on a table. Use the bowl to trace a half-circle with chalk along the folded edge. This will be your neck hole—make sure it's large enough for your head to fit through. You may need to adjust, but this will give you the general shape.

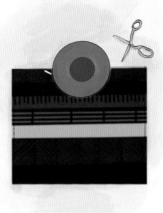

7. Cut out the traced neck hole. Pin the unfolded bias tape around the neck hole, right sides together. Using backstitch (see page 49), sew ¼ inch (6 mm) from the edge of the neck holeto hold the bias tape in place (or use your sewing machine). Fold the wrong side of the bias tape over the neck hole, to the wrong side of the fabric.

8. Press the bias tape into place with the iron, then topstitch (see page 50) ¼ inch (6 mm) from the neck edge (or use your sewing machine). This will help the neck to stay intact and not stretch out or go wonky.

9. Pin the strips on all four corners of the top's short ends and, using backstitch (see page 49), sew securely in place being sure that the diagnal ends of the wider strips point outward.

This top looks great with almost everything, especially skirts, shorts, and pants that are high-waisted. Make it again and put your own spin on it. Use muslin and make your own print using fabric paint and stamps—try an Ankara print with contrasting straps, or rethink the neckline!

In the 1950s, Black fashion designer Zelda Wynn Valdes's gowns were on-trend. Some were fitted and short and others loose and free. Girls started to wear more separates and many garments had cinched waists. Make your own separates by starting with this fifties inspired wrap top. Then read about the amazing Zelda on page 106!

► Create your own label inside your clothing. You can do this simply by sewing in a piece of ribbon or you can buy iron-on labels at the fabric store. This will help you identify the front from the back, and it gives it a professional pop (especially if you plan to sell it)!

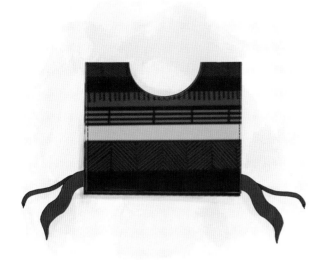

FAUX-FUR VEST

My mom loves her luxurious fur coats. When she wears them, it's instant elegance, and it brings out her inner diva. In the summer she stores them away so they are ready to go when the winter chill hits. Her mother, Cora, owned several furs, too. As a child, I remember secretly going into the basement of our family house to sneak a glance at them with my cousins. Viewing these personal investments was like finding a hidden treasure and memory. I did not inherit my mother's love for fur (I'll only rock it if it's vintage), but I understand why they are a point of joy and pride for many Black women.

Faux fur is fun, cozy, inexpensive, and it gives a sumptuous texture to your look! Similar to regular fur, if you take care of it, it will last forever, so you can pass it to a younger sister or your best friend when you're done being chic in it.

Materials

- Pattern (page 174) or loose-fitting T-shirt
- Pattern paper
- Pencil
- 1 yard (1 m) faux fur
- 1 yard (1 m) cotton, for lining

- Basic sewing supplies—needle, fabric scissors, thread, pins
- Sewing machine with sewing thread to match your fabric (optional)

Instructions

1. Use the pattern on page 174, and lay it on top of the pattern paper. (Alternatively, you can use a loose-fitting T-shirt; fold the shirt in half vertically and lay it on top of the pattern paper, trace around the shirt leaving off the sleeves.) Outline the entire shape about ¼ inch (6 mm) outside the first line, to give you seam allowance. Repeat for the front pattern piece, following the lower neckline. Cut out both pattern pieces on the outside line.

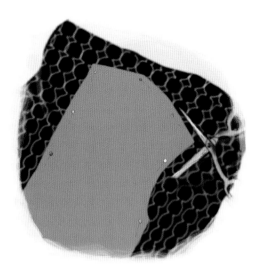

2. Using the pattern pieces, cut out the vest front twice out of the fur and lining. When cutting out the fur, place your pattern right side up on the fabric's wrong side. This will make it easier to cut. For the back pieces, fold the fabric and align the center of the pattern piece on the fold; this will give you one large piece. When you are done cutting, you should have six pieces total, three in each fabric.

3. Trim the fur. In order to sew the fur properly, use small scissors (if you have them) to trim the fur in the seam allowances. This will help with pinning and sewing the lining later.

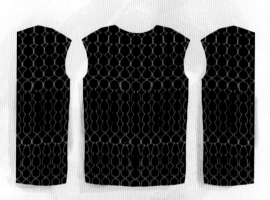

4. Lay the fur pieces right sides together, aligning the side seams and, using backstitch (see page 49), sew the side seams (or use your sewing machine). Repeat with the lining pieces.

5. Open up the fur and lining pieces and place them right sides together. Pin in place, pushing the fur to the inside. Leave the tops of the shoulders and 4 inches (10 cm) at the bottom of the vest open and, using backstitch (see page 49), sew around the rest of the vest, carefully tucking in any fur bits as you go along (or use your sewing machine).

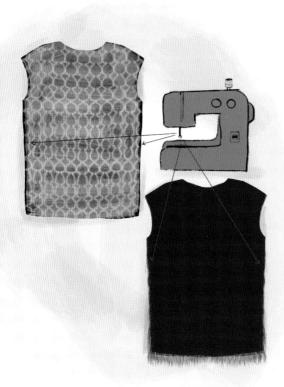

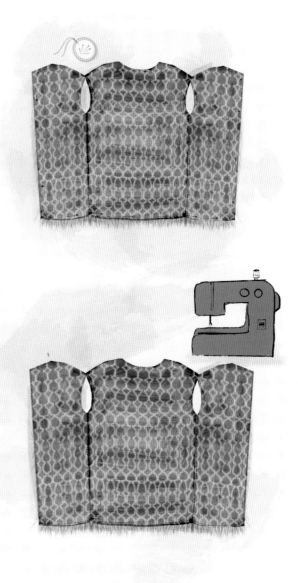

6. Turn the vest right side out through the opening at the bottom. Tuck the edges of the opening neatly to the inside, pin them in place, and sew the hole shut using an overcast stitch (see page 50).

7. Turn the vest so the lining fabric is on the outside. Flatten the shoulder openings and, using a running stitch (see page 49), sew them each closed, with an ⅛-inch (3 mm) seam allowance. Then sew the shoulder seams together. Turn the fur to the outside, and you're all done!

Warning: This project is lots of fun but can be messy. Make sure you have your broom and a dustpan nearby. You may want to give your vest a shake outside to free any stray bits of fur.

MORE WAYS TO MAKE

Make a matching fur zipper pouch with the scraps.

Materials

- Fur and lining scraps
- 7-inch (18 cm) zipper
- Basic sewing supplies—needle, fabric scissors, thread, pins
- Sewing machine with sewing thread to match your fabric (optional)

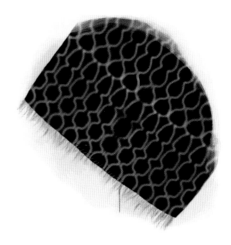

Instructions

1. Cut a 9 inch × 7 inch (23 cm × 18 cm) rectangle out of the lining and the fur. Trim the fur down for ¼ inch (6 mm) along the edges to create the seam allowances.

2. Place the lining and the fur wrong sides together. With the zipper teeth facing the right side of the liner, align one side of the zipper tape along one short end of the rectangle. Using a tight backstitch (see page 49), sew the zipper tape to the seam allowance (or use your sewing machine). Repeat on the opposite end of the rectangle with the other side of the zipper.

3. Fold the rectangle in half so the zipper is at the top with right sides of the lining together. Using a tight backstitch, sew along the side seams (or use your sewing machine). Turn the pouch right side out through the zippered opening.

DENIM GLOW UP

Denim is always great and you can wear it in *sew* many ways. It's sturdy and is easy to cut and embellish any way you like. Here, you will make over a garment in your closet or one that you've thrifted by adding applique, trim, and patches to customize.

Get ready to sew and say "what's up" to this denim jacket glow!

Materials

- Pencil and paper
- Denim jacket
- 1 yard (1 m) trim
- Tracing paper
- ¼ yard (23 cm) cotton fabric (for creating applique—everything matches denim, so pick a fabric that goes with your personality!)
- 4 to 5 patches

- Fusible bonding tape (Stitch Witchery or Dritz Bonding Web)
- Iron
- Fabric paint, bleach, etc. (optional)
- Basic sewing supplies—needle, fabric scissors, thread, pins
- Sewing machine with sewing thread to match your fabric (optional)

Instructions

1. Plan out your project. For ours, we're going to include a trim on the collar, letter appliques, and patches. Grab a pencil and paper and start designing. You might want to make a mini mood board to gather your thoughts. Figure out the theme for your jacket and put it on paper. Consider all the embellishment techniques on pages 141–148, such as stamping, bleach dyeing, stenciling, fringe, applique, quilting, and beading. Take your time with this part of the process. Ask for opinions. Have fun!

2. Select a trim that will improve the look of the jacket and add a special flair. Neatly sew the trim to your collar by hand, using an overcast stitch or a tight running stitch (see pages 49–50). Use a thread that matches your denim so it is not visible.

3. To create the letter applique, use your favorite font; make sure it's a bold typeface so that it's easy to trace and read. Figure out your phrase, print it out at the size you want, trace the letters onto tracing paper. Cut them out; these will be your pattern pieces.

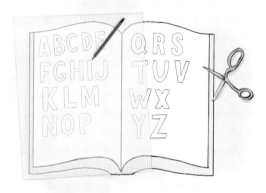

4. Pin your patterns to the cotton fabric and cut each letter out.

5. Place the fusible bonding material on the back of the fabric letters, trimming it so none of the fusible bonding material peeks around the edges of the letters, or you may get the glue on your iron. Follow the instructions on the package to fuse each letter onto your jacket. Make sure everything is smooth and flat on the jacket.

6. Play around with positioning the letters on the back of your jacket. Find the center of the back of your jacket and evenly place the letters on each side. They look good on a curve. Place the patches where they will go. Pin them in place. Carefully try your jacket on to see if you like it (don't get stuck on a pin!). Make sure you like the layout before moving forward.

7. Iron on the patches, if they have a fusible backing. Then sew them in place by hand using topstitch, or zigzag with your machine.

8. Topstitch (page 50) neatly around each of the letters by hand or zigzag with your machine.

Add any other embellishments based on your design sketch. Pay attention, know when to pull back, and always edit yourself. It's easy to go overboard. Apply your good taste and sensibilities!

Tip: Snip the sleeves: If the sleeves on your jacket are not working for you, cut them off to create a denim vest. These look great over long-sleeved tops and dresses.

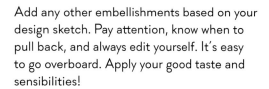

129

A HISTORIC BIT ON DENIM

Caroline A. Jones, author of *Machine in the Studio: Constructing the Postwar American Artist* wrote: "It took Martin Luther King's march on Washington to make them popular. . . . It was here that civil rights activists were photographed wearing the poor sharecropper's blue denim overalls to dramatize how little had been accomplished since Reconstruction."

Jeans have had a long history with Blacks in America. Prior to sharecropping days, denim was referred to as "clothes for negros." Sharecropping was an arrangement spanning from 1890 into the 1900s where the planter, usually a slave owner, allowed the tenant, usually a former slave, to use land in exchange for a share of the crop (a flawed system in which sharecroppers were often forcefully held in ways that were similar to slavery). Slave owners dressed the enslaved workers in this material because it was durable, would not tear, and helped to contrast them against the fancy dress of whites on the plantation. Denim dress was used as a dividing factor.

For decades the children of sharecroppers wore suits, ties, and hats to work their factory jobs. Many Blacks believed wearing denim was a sign of disrespect to themselves and the struggles of the past.

Thankfully the moment where denim represented painful reminders of the slavery and sharecropper system has (mostly) passed for Blacks in America. Now we wear denim, share denim, and love denim while writing new narratives. Denim is worn by people all over the world and is made by thousands of manufacturers across the globe. It is popular everywhere.

RAG DOLL

Rag dolls are a joy to make and full of magic. They are one of the oldest toys in existence because they could be easily made by simply reusing scraps. Create a rag doll that resembles you, dressed in a mini version of a project you've made from this book, or else one that you'd want to have or share with a friend.

Materials

- ¼ yard (23 cm) medium-weight cotton fabric in your skin tone color (another option is using muslin and dyeing it with coffee grounds or tea)
- Pattern (page 175)
- Stuffing (or you can use fabric scraps cut small)
- Fabric scraps
- Fabric paint or permanent markers (optional)
- 1 skein of yarn close to the color of your hair
- Scrap paper
- Basic sewing supplies—needle, fabric scissors, thread, pins
- Sewing machine with sewing thread to match your fabric (optional)

Instructions

1. Fold the fabric in half, right sides together. Pin the pattern pieces on top and cut as follows:

2. For the body: Cut once, creating two pieces—one piece will be the front and the other is the back.

3. For the arms and legs: Cut twice, creating eight pieces—four for the arms and four for the legs.

4. Place the body pieces right sides together. Using a running stitch (see page 49) and thread the color of the skin tone, sew ¼ inch (6 mm) away from the edge all the way around, leaving about 1 inch (2.5 cm) open on one side (or use your sewing machine).

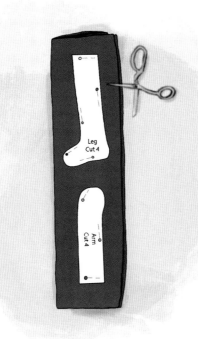

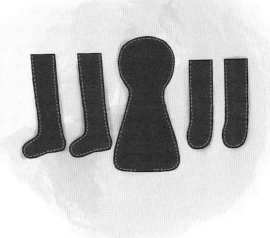

5. Sew the arms and legs together next; you will need to sew each piece with the right sides of the fabric facing, leaving the top end on each unsewn. Clip the curves and turn inside out. You will need to sew a total of four pieces—two legs and two arms.

7. Fold over the open ends of each limb. Pin the arms and legs to the body and, using backstitch, sew them in place using thread the color of the skin tone.

6. Stuff the arms and legs. You can use stuffing if you have it, or small fabric scraps to fill it. You want the limbs to be firm. Use a chopstick or a pencil to assist with pushing the stuffing into your doll parts.

8. Stuff the doll's body and, using a running stitch (see page 49), sew the opening closed.

9. Using the illustration on page 139, make a proportional face for your doll. Carefully use your fabric marker, paint, or stitching to create it. Before you put markers or paint on your fabric, make sure you test how it looks by making a sample on a scrap piece. If you want to keep it simple, you could use small buttons for the eyes and a heart applique for the mouth.

10. Now that the doll is assembled, it's time to add the hair. There are several styles you can make. We are going to give our doll pigtails. Start by measuring the back of the doll's head, from the top seam to the base of her neck. Using this measurement, cut your yarn into 11-inch (28 cm) pieces. You'll need to cut enough so that when the yarns are lined up they equal the head measurement.

11. Next, grab some scrap paper and sandwich the yarn in between two pieces, keeping the yarns in a line. Using thread that matches the color of the hair, with a topstitch (see page 50) sew through the paper across the center of the yarns, creating a part in the "hair" with the stitches. Remove the paper by gently pulling it from the stitching. Then, using thread that matches the hair, attach the hair to the doll with a toptstitch, starting at the head seam and going down the center of the back of the head.

12. After all the pieces of yarn are sewn in place, you can make two ponytails. Tie them off with a piece of contrasting yarn or ribbon and trim them to the desired length. Now your rag doll has hair! Maybe you'll make her a hair accessory—like a scrunchie (page 61)!

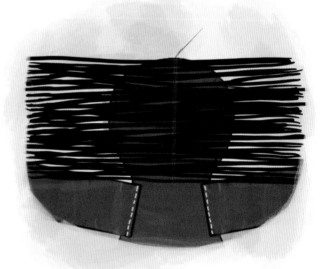

Now that your doll is constructed, it is time to make mini clothes using your scraps. Be creative, use your imagination and what you've learned from other projects on previous pages, and have fun!

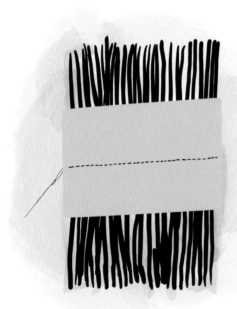

EMBELLISHMENTS

DAZZLE YOUR FASHION

Take the time to explore the magic of embellishment and surface design. Surface design and embellishment are all around us. If you look in the space you are in right now or at what you are wearing, I bet you can find inspiration. Notice the pillow on your sofa, plants, prints in the painting on the wall, or even your outfit! Here are a few techniques that have roots in the Black arts-and-crafts tradition.

Materials

- 11-inch × 11-inch (28 cm × 28 cm) squares of fabric (material will depend on which technique you are trying: muslin, white cotton, denim, canvas, or printed cotton)

- Basic sewing supplies—needle, fabric scissors, thread, pins
- Additional materials listed within each technique.

STAMP PRINTING

This printing method is simple and fun to do. Practice with some stamps, if you have some, and then figure out how you can create Ankara-like prints yourself. If you don't have stamps you can use found items around your home like a pencil's eraser or the top of a nail polish bottle.

Look at your favorite fabric prints for inspiration. Try to create interesting varying/repeating patterns.

Materials

- Block-printing ink
- Foam plate
- Small sponge (you can cut up a dish sponge)
- Stamps
- Cardboard
- Any material fabric square

Instructions

1. Pour a small amount of ink onto your plate and dip the small sponge into the ink.

2. Use the sponge to evenly cover the stamp's design in ink by tapping it on and shaking off any excess.

3. Place a piece of cardboard under your square of fabric. This will prevent ink from bleeding through to your work surface.

4. Press the stamp down on the fabric firmly, then lift straight up from the fabric, not at an angle.

5. Reload your stamp with ink using the sponge, and continue to apply the print, lifting straight up to prevent ink from going to the places you don't want it.

Don't worry about messing up—the beauty of this is in the handcrafted look!

PROJECTS TO TRY THIS TECHNIQUE WITH

- ▶ Ankara Triangle Reversible Headwrap (page 65)
- ▶ Reusable Face Mask (page 75)
- ▶ No-Waste Waist Bag (page 81)
- ▶ Vintage-Inspired Wrap Top (page 111)

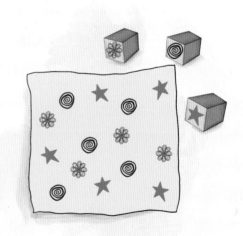

BLEACH DYE

Removing color with bleach is so simple. Spray the bleach and see what kinds of artsy pieces you create!

Materials

- Old clothes
- Protective mask
- Disposable gloves
- 16-ounce (470-ml) spray bottle
- Bleach
- Denim or dark-colored fabric squares (use natural fibers)
- Cardboard stencils, leaves, and shapes to place on top of your fabric (optional)
- Rubber bands

Instructions

1. This project works best outdoors on a flat surface or somewhere that can be washed with water after completion, like a bathtub. Put on old clothes, a mask, and gloves.

2. Fill a spray bottle with 10 ounces (300 ml) cold tap water and 5 ounces (150 ml) bleach.

3. Lay the fabric flat on your work surface.

4. Spray the bleach mixture on the fabric in any pattern or design you want to try. See what happens if you change how close you are to the fabric or how far away—you can go minimal or max depending on your project and style! Experiment with placing stencils or leaves on top of the fabric, twisting rubber bands around the fabric to hide areas from the bleach (this is called resist dyeing), or spraying the fabric on both sides.

5. Let the piece sit for five to ten minutes, then have an adult wash and dry the fabric.

Consider ways to use this as a technique to upcycle things you already have!

PROJECTS TO TRY THIS TECHNIQUE WITH

- Denim Scrunchie (page 61)
- Scrap Earrings (page 71)
- Reusable Face Mask (page 75)
- No-Waste Waist Bag (page 81)
- Denim Glow Up (page 125)

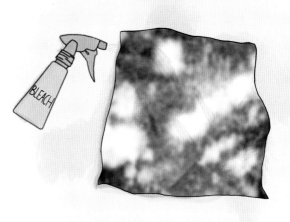

FABRIC MARKER WITH STENCILS

A stencil is a cutout shape or design on paper, plastic, or metal. Marker or paint is applied through the cutout to create the design that gets printed on the piece—in this case, fabric!

Materials

- Stencils (at least 1 inch/2.5 cm large, depending on the scale of the project)
- Canvas or white cotton fabric squares
- Cardboard
- Masking tape
- Ruler (optional)
- Pencil
- Fabric markers or paint and paintbrush

Instructions

1. Figure out what stencil(s) you want to put on your fabric square.

2. Place a piece of cardboard under your square of fabric. This will prevent ink from bleeding through to your work surface.

3. Use masking tape or your ruler and pencil to mark guidelines for placing your design if you want.

4. Trace your stencils with pencil and then color your design in with markers or paint.

PROJECTS TO TRY THIS TECHNIQUE WITH

- ▶ Ankara Triangle Reversible Headwrap (page 65)
- ▶ Black Girls Sew Tote (page 91)
- ▶ Vintage-Inspired Wrap Top (page 111)
- ▶ Denim Glow Up (page 125)

FRINGE

Fringe is fab! In the 1920s, during the Harlem Renaissance, it was used to make entire dresses—now fringe is fun in big and small ways! Use it as a pop to finish off a project. You can also easily turn a fringe into tassels.

Materials

- Assorted fabric squares
- Chalk
- Tape
- Ruler or tape measure
- Fabric scissors

Instructions

1. Determine the length you want your fringe to be. (We believe the longer the better.) You can always give it a trim to fit your style after it's attached.

2. Place your square of material on a flat surface. Use your chalk and ruler to mark lines every ½ inch (1.3 cm). Place a piece of tape the length of the fabric along one edge, perpendicular to the chalk lines, so you know where to stop cutting.

3. Cut the fringe along the lines, stopping at the tape. Stretch out the strips after you cut them. They should begin to curl on the sides, looking more like fringe. Remove the tape and the fringe strip is done!

Keep testing the fabric to make sure it will not fray too much. You may have to give it a good shake to get rid of the excess fibers. Now try this with a bigger piece of fabric, or even a real or faux leather, and sew it on to one of your projects.

PROJECTS TO TRY THIS TECHNIQUE WITH

- ▶ Wear a Crown (page 55)
- ▶ No-Waste Waist Bag (page 81)
- ▶ Fashion Capital Sweatshirt (page 103)
- ▶ Faux-Fur Vest (page 117)
- ▶ Denim Glow Up (page 125)

REVERSE APPLIQUE

— — — — — — — — — — —

Reverse applique is essentially the opposite of regular applique (like in the Fashion Capital Sweatshirt, page 103, and Denim Glow Up, page 125). Shapes are cut from the top fabric, revealing another piece of fabric underneath. This is a great way to add texture and unexpected detail.

Materials

- Fabric square
- Fabric for reverse applique (that goes underneath)
- Thread to match your main fabric square
- Basic sewing supplies—needle, fabric scissors, thread, pins

Instructions

1. Draw the applique design on the main square of fabric using a pencil or chalk. Outline the design about ¼ inch (6 mm) outside the initial lines.

2. Cut the shape out following the inner outline. Snip any curves around to create ease, but do not cut beyond the outer design line.

3. Fold the fabric under along the outside design line and finger press. Place the applique fabric underneath. Neatly hand-stitch around the opening with an overcast stitch or running stitch (see pages 49–50).

4. Press.

PROJECTS TO TRY THIS TECHNIQUE WITH

- ► Scrap Earrings (page 71)
- ► Reusable Face Mask (page 75)
- ► Vintage-Inspired Wrap Top (page 111)
- ► Denim Glow Up (page 125)

SCRAPPY (IMPROV) QUILTING

Black women and quilting date back to slavery. This was a highly skilled job, and the quilts they produced were in constant demand by wealthy families. Members of the Underground Railroad placed hidden symbols in their quilts as roadmaps to help slaves escape. Quilting is woven into our history—what is the story you will tell with your scraps to make a one-of-a-kind quilt? The idea here is to make a small quilted piece that can be used in a larger project. Maybe you turn this quilted square into a pocket on the outside of your tote bag. Or you frame it as a gift to a friend! For a full-size quilt you would need a lot more material and a lot more time—we're just here to embellish.

Materials

- Fabric scraps
- Cotton squares
- Batting (you can use any fluffy fabric)

Instructions

1. Using a running stitch (see page 49), sew fabric scraps together, right sides facing, using a ¼-inch (6 mm) seam allowance. Keep adding more scraps until they create a fabric the same size as your fabric square. You can make the piece bigger and then cut it down to the same dimensions. Sewing together the scraps to make a square is called "piecing."

2. Place the cotton square on your work surface right side down. Place a piece of batting cut to the same size on top. Place your pieced square right side up on top of the stack. This is called a "quilt sandwich."

3. Using a small running stitch (see page 49) or your machine, sew straight lines across the fabric to hold the pieces together—this is what's called "quilting." Sew several lines until the square becomes a puffy block.

For your next quilt block, play around with the quilting lines you create. Try squiggles, waves, or zigzags.

PROJECTS TO TRY THIS TECHNIQUE WITH

▸ Denim Scrunchie (page 61)
▸ Ankara Triangle Reversible Headwrap (page 65)
▸ Fashion Capital Sweatshirt (page 103)
▸ Denim Glow Up (page 125)
▸ Rag Doll (page 133)

SIMPLE BEADING

Beads in your hair, beads around your wrist—let's try beads on fabric. Beading is a wonderful way to accent and give a personalized touch to truly make a project your own.

Beadwork has been a part of the African tradition for many thousands of years—the first beads were made from natural materials like bones, seeds, or shells. All over the continent, beadwork was used in many ways as a form of communication. My favorite example is women and men wearing beads to indicate their status, and that they had passed rites of passage. Today's beads are typically made from glass, wood, or plastic.

Materials

- Thread that matches your fabric
- The smallest needle you have
- Ankara or other printed or solid cotton fabric square
- Bugle or seed beads (depending on the project you hope to make, 25–30)
- 8-inch (20 cm) embroidery hoop (optional)

Instructions

1. Determine the area of the fabric you will bead. It is very pretty to add beads to a certain section of a print; for example, if you are working with a fabric that has animals on it, maybe you use them on the eyes. This is a great way to add a little sparkle!

2. Thread your needle and tie a knot.

3. Bring the needle through the back of the fabric, place a bead on the needle, go back down into the fabric, sew two running stitches (see page 49 to secure the bead in place), bring the needle to the front of the fabric, place another bead, and repeat, placing the beads how you like.

4. Tie a double knot when you are done sewing to prevent your hard work from coming undone.

This is a meticulous process, but it can have beautiful results. If you have the patience to bead, you can do anything!

PROJECTS TO TRY THIS TECHNIQUE WITH

- ▶ Wear a Crown (page 55)
- ▶ Scrap Earrings (page 71)
- ▶ Reusable Face Mask (page 75)
- ▶ Tulle Tutu (page 97)
- ▶ Denim Glow Up (page 125)

4. SEW,

WHAT'S NEXT?

Now it's time to put some of what you've learned into action to have a positive impact on sewing and the future of fashion. Maybe you have found a way to speak up verbally or with what you wear. Maybe you want to tackle an issue you've discovered. If you feel frustrated about something, you are not the only one. Use your voice: Your activism can be quiet, like a quote on a Black Girls Sew tote, or loud, like educating others on the history of Black people in the fashion industry.

Here are some ideas on how to make a positive change in your own way. Try some of the suggestions on the pages that follow to expand your circle, have an impact, and grow. Remember, even the smallest change can be big.

You are powerful!

Supercharge Your Fashion Future

Create Your Community

Identify your sewing friends and create your #fashionteam. Find others who have a similar style to yours and create a fashion club at school, church, or virtually. It's easier to build when your voices are together. You don't have to go it alone. Use your energy to bring others along. If you see someone who has talent or cares about a common cause, invite them in. Look for people who see you and your value. It will take time, but find your groove and work within it.

Promote, Style, and Sell

Produce a Fashion Show: Fashion shows are events that fashion designers organize to debut their latest collection of clothing or accessories. Figure out the date—do you want to have it during traditional Fashion Week (in February or September), in advance of going back to school, or over holidays? Select your models, music, the venue, and theme. Design the program and runway decor, and get to it! Then write out your run of show, or the order that events will happen in. In this rundown, include everything like when the models will arrive, when the welcome will happen, when the music will start, the order that the models will walk—every last detail.

Tip: On page 156, you'll learn about Eunice Johnson—pretend you are producing an Ebony Fashion Fair show! Look up videos on YouTube to find inspiration. Create a mood board to help others better understand the vibe you would like to create at your show.

Have a Photo Shoot: Photo shoots are fun and can be as simple as going around your block with a friend to get good shots. You do not need a fancy camera or special lighting. A mobile phone and natural light from the sun will do. Most mobile devices have editing software you can download for free to help you tweak the images to your liking. Here are a few additional tricks to make sure you get the best pics:

- Use the back camera for the highest resolution if you are shooting with your phone. The resolution has a direct impact on the quality of your images and is especially important if you will be printing them.
- Leave lots of negative space. Negative space is the space around and between the models in a photo. This technique is most interesting when it forms an artsy shape. You may notice that the model's silhouette in the garment looks amazing if they are posing a certain way.
- Shoot off-center. Photos look more fab when they are not perfectly centered. Try placing your subject in different parts of the frame to see what results you get.
- Have a shot list. This is the list of things you want to capture. So make a list of the projects from this book that you are shooting and the angles you want to get, for example, profiles, birds-eye, detail shots (like a button), up close, or straight on.

When you're done you can use the photos to publish a lookbook, zine, or a learning portfolio.

- A lookbook is a collection of photographs compiled to show off the talent of a model, photographer, stylist, or items of clothing.
- A zine is a small published book of original artwork and words usually printed on a photocopier in small amounts, for example, ten to fifteen copies.
- A learning portfolio is a collection of process and final project photos used to help when applying to art-focused high schools, colleges, apprenticeships, or internships.

Host a Pop-Up Shop or Clothing Swap: A pop-up shop is a short-term sales space. Create a pop-up that features some of the accessories, clothing, or home decor (like pillows and dolls) that you make. Present things in an interesting way—this is called "merchandising." This can be a lot of fun, and a great way to learn about sales.

If you don't have enough inventory to do a pop-up shop, coordinate a clothing swap! A clothing swap is a party where each of your guests brings a few pieces of gently used, clean clothing or accessories. The items are free for anyone to take so you can "shop" for what you want to get new clothing for your wardrobe or to upcycle, while sewing, without spending any money! How fun! Any remaining clothing at the end of the event can be donated to nonprofit organizations like Goodwill, or a homeless shelter. A win-win.

Hidden Figure of Fashion:

EUNICE JOHNSON

(1916–2010)

A savvy businesswoman who used her influence to advocate for inclusion in fashion and beauty, Eunice Johnson created Ebony Fashion Fair in 1958, a runway show highlighting Black models and designers. She was also one of the first to launch a cosmetics line for dark skin.

Johnson was born Eunice Walker in Selma, Alabama, the setting for the Civil Rights Movement in the sixties and where the Montgomery marches began. Her father was a doctor and her mother was a high school principal. Johnson was one of four children. She graduated with a degree in sociology from Talladega College in 1938, and then with a master's degree in social work from Loyola University in Chicago. During her college years, she joined the sorority Delta Sigma Theta—which Lesley is a member of! She met her husband, John H. Johnson, while at a formal dance in 1940.

Eunice and John founded *Ebony* magazine, for Black readers, in 1945. It was Eunice's idea to name the magazine after fine-grain dark wood. As the magazine grew, Eunice noticed the lack of opportunity for non-whites in fashion. They could only be found in publications like her own.

This inspired her to create the Ebony Fashion Fair as a fundraiser for a hospital. The fashion show tour would ultimately expand and visit more than two hundred cities across the United States, Canada, and the Caribbean between 1958–2009. Eunice was pleased to see the show expand from just benefitting a single organization to raising over $55 million for several Black charities. The show created space for Black models and the works of Black designers. Eunice orchestrated hundreds of fabulous runway shows, held on Sunday afternoons, where the women and girls in attendance wore their very best. Lesley remembers attending these shows as a girl with her mom and sitting in awe of the extravagant fashion.

Eunice also took notice at that time of how difficult it was to find cosmetics, especially foundation, that was the right hue for the skin tones of her models. So with the support of her husband, she developed and launched Fashion Fair Cosmetics in 1973, creating a line of makeup that was sold in major department stores.

In the 1960s, Black stylists and editors were not allowed to borrow clothing from luxury houses like Valentino to use in editorial magazine shoots or fashion shows, as was a common practice for white stylists at the time. Eunice did not let this stop her—she demanded the main houses let her borrow their pieces, and pushed even further by convincing these luxury houses to start using Black models in their shows. Eunice told the *New York Times* in 2001, "I was in Paris, and I told Valentino: 'If you can't find any black models, we'll get some for you. And if you can't use them, we're not going to buy from you anymore.'"

A pioneer and entrepreneurial trailblazer, Eunice Johnson made a permanent beauty mark on fashion. Her legacy lives on through the many businesswomen she has inspired to beautifully go for their dreams.

Your Sewing & Fashion Career

You learned from the hidden figures in fashion profiles that being Black and working in fashion has had its pros and lots of cons, but even when we were not treated as equals, we did not let that stop us. We were always willing to make the dress, start the project, partner with others, and help where we could. The reality is that our ambition alone cannot dismantle years of racism, but conversations are being had and change is happening. The book you are reading is an example of things getting better. The power is in your hands.

You are young and there is no rush, but we suggest you familiarize yourself with careers in sewing and fashion. This will help you to get your foot in the door when it is time to explore. Not only will this give you an advantage, it will help you and your parents understand that fashion can be a career option. Many Black immigrant and first-generation families may not understand this, leading girls to go into careers that they are not passionate about, just to make a living.

Follow people in careers you are interested in on social media to get a sense of their lives. Keep doing your homework and learning more. By spending time educating yourself, you will be able to get past the gatekeepers—or better yet, create your own gate.

Always, always, try to lift as you climb. We need to see ourselves in all areas of the world, so help your fellow Black Girl sewists and fashionistas as much as you can.

These are a few other things you can do:

- Learn how to send professional emails. If you cannot send a good email, you are in trouble. Period. This is how work gets done in every facet of fashion.
- Make a list of places where you could intern while in high school—like at a fabric store, with an independent designer, at a fashion company, or at a boutique. When you go on interviews for these internships, make sure you ask questions about the company, the work you'll be doing, and if that person enjoys working there.
- Practice talking about your work. Describe things like what you were inspired by, materials used, and what makes it unique.
- Find a sewing or fashion mentor. Your sewing mentor could be someone in your community who sews and knows you want to learn and is willing to support and challenge you and your abilities. They may not be easy to find but taking a class and joining a sewing community are the best ways to connect with them. It is a wonderful feeling when your deepest potential is seen by someone who is on a path that you would like to pursue. Stay connected and keep in touch.
- Learn more about the fashion capitals, because everything does not have to happen in America. Study the cities (see the list on page 103) and then find opportunities to travel around the world! Go abroad with family, virtually, or through school or student travel organizations.

- Continue to sew and take in all the sewing education you can. Enroll in camps, attend pre-college programs, get private instruction, or take a class at a local fabric store. If you look you will find it; if you don't find it in your community, create it. Assemble your own group and get together to watch videos on YouTube or educational platforms like CreativeBug.
- Read more (and more) books about fashion designers, fashion trends, and sewing.
- Take notes!

Use your talent to break down walls if you want, or just be in the know. Either way, you are impacting the future of fashion.

It is hard to believe that we still often hear the phrase "first Black woman to . . ."

You have learned about six people, mostly women, in fashion who were the first to do something. They endured many struggles but also experienced joy and success. What attributes do they have in common? Is it their grace, business savvy, or courage? How do you think they were able to dig deep into the power that already exists inside them? In your fashion journal, make a note about this, or what you found to be dissimilar. What did you learn? How does this inspire you?

Maintain Your Balance

Playing, eating well, sleeping a lot, taking long baths, being involved in your community, doing well in school, wearing what makes you glow, giving back, creating (of course), and resting are ways to add balance to your life! These actions are all a part of self-care. It is important! Always remember to take care of yourself and eliminate what doesn't make you happy.

Set healthy boundaries around your time and talents. Protect yourself. Honor your creativity.

Are you inspired to let your sewing and fashion superpowers shine through? We need a new thing in fashion—and that new thing is you! Bring your contributions and tell your unique story.

If you
Believe in yourself.
Stay open-minded.
Optimize opportunity.
The possibilities will be endless (for you).

Over generations, we have cared for ourselves, and others, with fashion—and look at where we are now. I hope you can see, by looking into fashion's past, that we were already in the future. Ahead of the times. Thinking beyond circumstances. It is what we do. So work in your own way, at your own pace. The power is in our hands: Tap into your magic and keep sewing!

GLOSSARY

Accessories: Articles or items of clothing carried or worn to complement a garment or outfit

Aesthetics: The nature of beauty and taste

Applique: A small piece of fabric attached by hand or machine to a larger piece of fabric to create a design, e.g., patches

Black Girl Magic: A movement that celebrates the beauty, power, and resilience of Black women started by CaShawn Thompson

Black Girls Sew: An organization founded by Hekima Hapa with the intent of having a positive impact on the lives of youth and families through education in sewing, design, and entrepreneurship

Bespoke: Designed for a specific audience, like kidswear, bridal, menswear, etc. Example: That tailor makes bespoke clothing for kids.

Chic: Stylish or 🔥

Croquis: The French word for "sketch," used to refer to the fashion figure

Deadstock: Inventory from clothing companies that does not sell and might not sell in the future but is still in new condition

Details: The separate parts of a look as they relate to the whole

DIY: Do It Yourself

Embellish(ment): Adding decoration to something, like patches or trim

Fashion: The prevailing style of the time. Also, an expression of self, creativity, or an idea through clothing

Fashion designer: A person whose job is to come up with ideas for new clothing designs

Faux: The French word for "fake"

Fibers: The raw material that makes a fabric. Fibers can be natural or synthetic.

Garment: An article of clothing

Headwear: An accessory that is worn on the head, like a crown or headwrap (see pages 55 and 65.)

Hem: A sewing method that involves folding and sewing the edge of a fabric to keep it from unraveling. This usually happens at the bottom of a garment or the ends of sleeves.

Home goods: Items and products used within homes, like pillows, quilts, rag dolls, etc.

Hue: A quality of color that distinguishes one color from another

160

Inspiration: Something or someone that gives you an idea, like a mood board.

Lining: Inner layer of fabric

Merchandise: Goods to be bought and sold

Mood board: A collection of visuals that evoke a concept or style

Normalize: To become a standard condition or state

Organic: Produced without the use of chemical fertilizers, pesticides, or other artificial agents

Pattern: This word has two meanings in sewing: paper in the shape of the parts of a garment or accessory accompanied by a set of instructions to cut and sew garments, accessories, and home décor; or a repeating motif, like dots or lightning bolts, on fabric.

Proportions: The size of various components in relation to the whole

Quality: The standard of a garment measured against other things of a similar kind; the degree of excellence of something.

Ready to wear: Clothing made for the general market and sold in stores/off the rack

Rhythm: Harmonious details often found in good design

Sewist: Or a seamstress; someone who sews. Also, a combination of sew and artist to describe someone who creates sewn art, including clothing or other items with sewing elements

Silhouette: The shape or outline of something

Stylist: A person whose job it is to put clothing and accessories together

Surface design: Any type of artwork like pattern, illustration, hand lettering, etc. made by a sewist that is applied to a textile surface to enhance its appearance

Sustainable fashion: A movement and process around mindful fashion production that encourages clothes and accessories to be made without harming the environment or the people who make them. Also known as green fashion.

Swatch: A small piece of fabric—ask for one the next time you visit a fabric store

Texture: The way a material feels or looks

Textile: Cloth—fabric, material

Textile industry: The manufacturing businesses related to design, production, and distribution of yarn, cloth, and clothing

Trim: Decorations that are used to embellish a garment

Trend: What's in fashion right now, and what's next in fashion

Upcycle: To use something that you would normally throw away

Zigzag: A machine stitch that looks like a string of Zs

ABOUT THE AUTHORS

HEKIMA HAPA

**Independent Fashion Designer,
Founder of Black Girls Sew**

Hekima searched the phrase "Black Girls Sew" in 2012 to find activities for her daughter, who was learning to sew. She noticed that all the image results were Black women working in garment factories or getting sewn-in hair weaves. Unhappy with this finding, she decided to make a change by starting Black Girls Sew, a Brooklyn-based nonprofit organization that teaches youth sewing, design, and entrepreneurship skills.

Hekima was born in Avon Park, Florida, a tiny town nicknamed "the city of charm." Hekima learned to sew from her mother at age twelve, admitting, "it was a necessity and not about being fashionable." One of twelve siblings, she comes from a big family and a long line of quilters and makers. Hekima observed that when you look good, people treat you better, even if you are poor. This sparked her interest in fashion and the rest is her-story!

In addition to founding Black Girls Sew, Hekima is a fashion designer at Harriet's by Hekima (HbyH). HbyH specializes in contemporary, ready-to-wear African fashion.

Hekima is committed to using her talents to impart life skills and everything she knows about green fashion through the process of sewing and fashion design.

Hekima's favorites:

- ► Music to listen to while sewing: Afrobeats (Burna Boy)
- ► Fabric type: Denim
- ► Snack: Herb-and-yeast popcorn
- ► Beverage to enjoy while sewing: Herbal iced tea
- ► Season to sew: Summer

LESLEY WARE

Author, Founder of
The Creative Cookie and Art to Ware

Similar to Hekima, Lesley was shopping in 2012 for a book to help with the sewing classes that she was starting to teach at the time. After looking in several stores and being unsuccessful at finding a book with any Black faces, the idea popped into her head to write a book. A few years later, in 2015, her first book, *Sew Fab: Sewing and Style for Young Fashionistas*, was published. This book is her fifth!

Lesley's mom taught her to sew when she was only four. They created fun costumes, dresses, and quilts together. Lesley took on all the small jobs—sewing on buttons, stuffing things, and doing the running stitch. One of her first memories is visiting a Joann fabric store in her tiny hometown of Muskegon, Michigan, to pick out materials and notions. She is an only child.

In addition to being an author of several books about sewing, fashion, and style for youth, her work involves teaching at several fashion-focused institutions in and outside of New York City. She also opened three socially conscious pop-up shops in 2021! When she has time, she loves to design.

Lesley truly believes that all of her work with young people, will give fashion a brighter future by lifting and amplifying their voices and new ideas.

Lesley's favorites:

- ► Sewing tool: Loop turner
- ► Music to listen to while sewing: Rihanna, Beyoncé, Billie Eilish
- ► Fabric type: Organic soft cotton
- ► Snack: Gummy bears and popcorn
- ► Beverage to enjoy while sewing: Iced coffee
- ► Season to sew: Spring

LAYLAH AMATULLAH BARRAYN

Photographer

Laylah Amatullah Barrayn is a documentary photographer from Brooklyn, New York. She is the co-author of the book *MFON: Women Photographers of the African Diaspora*, the first anthology in nearly thirty years that highlights photography produced by women of African descent. Her work was nominated for a 2020 News & Documentary Emmy Award. She is a frequent contributor to the *New York Times* and has been published in *National Geographic*, NPR, and *Vogue*, as well as other publications. Laylah went to college at NYU. As a girl her grandmother used to make all of her clothing, and that developed her love for fashion!

Photograph by Barnabas Crosby

MORGAN WIDMER

Illustrator

Morgan is a fashion designer and illustrator from West Virginia. She went to college for fashion design at West Virginia University and studied abroad twice at Central Saint Martins in London. She is the creator of her own sustainable clothing and accessories brand made entirely of scraps called Morgania. Morgan has also written and self-published her own cookbook, *Easy Yummies For Vegan Tummies*. She also does freelance illustrations related to fashion and art. Morgan's love for fashion began with never wanting to stop playing dress-up as a little girl, which has now been combined with her distaste for the way the fashion industry currently works—breeding her desire to help save the planet with beautiful, fun, and expressive sustainable fashion.

ACKNOWLEDGMENTS

We'd like to give a special shoutout to all of the amazing young women who modeled the projects in this book: Zinga Bellerice, Alanna Boateng, Kira Campbell, Zawditu Collymore, Sandra Davis, Queen Omega Lawerence, and Ziyah Sookhoo.

Shoutout to the Black girls I have encountered in my role as a fashion educator and author. You have challenged me, asked tough questions, and showed up in ways that have truly moved me forward and forced me to be better. This book is for YOU. I hope you love it! We need more of you as the next generation of makers, sewists, businesswomen, and designers. I pray that you never feel like you need to shrink or hide. Everything you want is within your grasp, so spread your magic, dream big, and grab it!

I also want to give a ginormous thank-you to:

Gwendolyn and Herbert Leslie Williams, my parents, for fostering my sense of taste and love of fabulous fashion.

Victor Varnado, my super-supportive husband, for having great ideas and making me crack up laughing all the time.

Cleo Zell, Nicole A. Taylor, and Shimira Williams, my closest friends while writing this book, who encouraged me, made me feel loved, and kept me motivated.

Morgan Widmer and Laylah Amatullah Barrayn for sharing their talents in illustration and photography to bring lots of interest and color to these pages.

Andrea R. Somberg, my agent, and Meredith A. Clark, my editor at Abrams, for helping me create yet another beautiful sewing activity book!

—Lesley

Give thanks to Most High and our ancestors who have sewn before us.

Special thanks to my mother, Rebecca Stukes, for empowering me with the most important skill of sewing.

To all our Sew Green Fashion Campers and family, our non-profit nor this book would not be possible with you. We have created an amazing set of projects to share with the world.

—Hekima

REFERENCES

Anti-Racist Guidebook. Social Justice Sewing Academy (2021).

Bailey, Ronald. "The Other Side of Slavery: Black Labor, Cotton, and Textile Industrializaition in Great Britain and the United States." *Agricultural History* (Spring 1994).

Bare, Eman. "Head Wraps Aren't Just a NYFW Accessory." *Teen Vogue* (September 15, 2017).

Deihl, Nancy. 2015. "A profile of Zelda Wynn Valdes: costume and fashion designer." *Oxford University Press* blog, March 31, 2015.

Dollar Times (website), n.d. "Calculate the Value of $1,000 in 1959." https://www.dollartimes.com/inflation/inflation.php?amount=1000&year=1959.

Edmunds, Alice. *Who Puts the Blue in Jeans.* Random House, 1976.

Gabbara, Princess. 2018. "How Zelda Wynn Valdes Redefined Fashion." *Shondaland* (website). April 25, 2018. https://www.shondaland.com/live/style/a19992024/zelda-wynn-valdes.

Gonzalez, David. 1994. "ABOUT NEW YORK; Matriarch of Dancers Sews Clothing of Delight." *New York Times*, March 23, 1994.

Jones, Caroline A. *Machine in the Studio: Constructing the Postwar American Artist.* Chicago and London: The University of Chicago Press, 1998.

Kai, Maiysha. 2018. "#ThrowbackThursday: The Legend of Zelda (Wynn Valdes)." *The Root* (website). May 17, 2018. https://www.theroot.com/throwbackthursday-the-legend-of-zelda-wynn-valdes-1826114814.

Lafuente, Maite and Aitana Lleonart. *Fashion Illustration: Figure Drawing.* Parragon Inc., 2007.

Missouri State Parks (website). n.d. "Textile Mills and daily Life in America at Watkins Woolen Mill State Historic Site." https://mostateparks.com/page/55168/textile-mills-and-daily-life-america.

Purnell, Brian and Jeanne Theoharis. 2017. "How New York City became the capital of the Jim Crow North." *Washington Post*, August 23, 2017.

Sanders, Jasmine. 2019. "A Black Legacy, Wrapped Up in Fur." *New York Times.* January 31, 2019.

Spears, Charlezine Wood. *How to Wear Colors: with Emphasis on Dark Skins*, Fourth Edition. Burgess Pub. Co, 1965.

Ware, Lesley. *Sew Fab: Sewing and Style for Young Fashionistas.* Laurence King Publishing, 2015.

Wikipedia, s.v. "*Playboy*," last modified on August 31, 2021, 16.56, https://en.wikipedia.org/wiki/Playboy#Rabbit_logo.

Wikipedia, s.v. "Zelda Wynn Valdes," last modified on September 16, 2021, 04:18, https://en.wikipedia.org/wiki/Zelda_Wynn_Valdes.

PARIS

Fashion Capital
Sweatshirt

Scrap Earrings

Reusable Face Mask

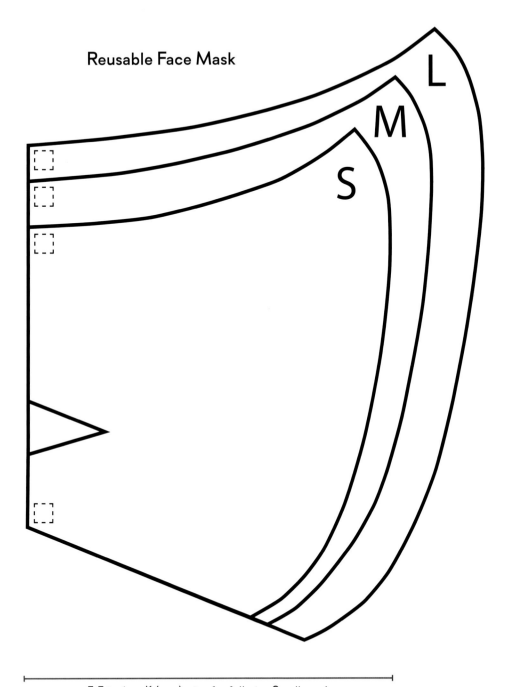

5.5 inches (14 cm), size for full-size Small mask

Faux-Fur Vest

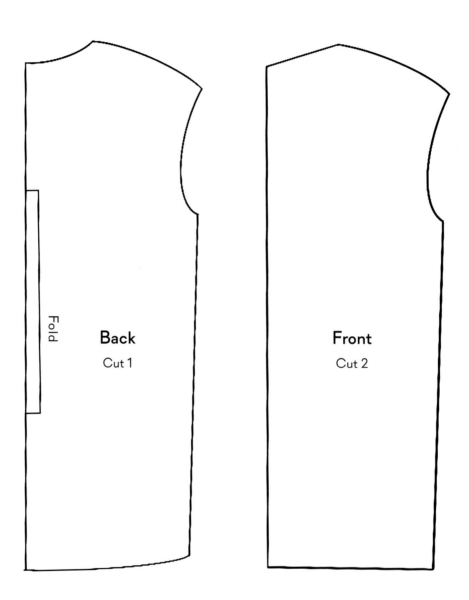

Back
Cut 1

Fold

Front
Cut 2

Note: Pattern is not to scale. When scanning and printing, enlarge to desired size.

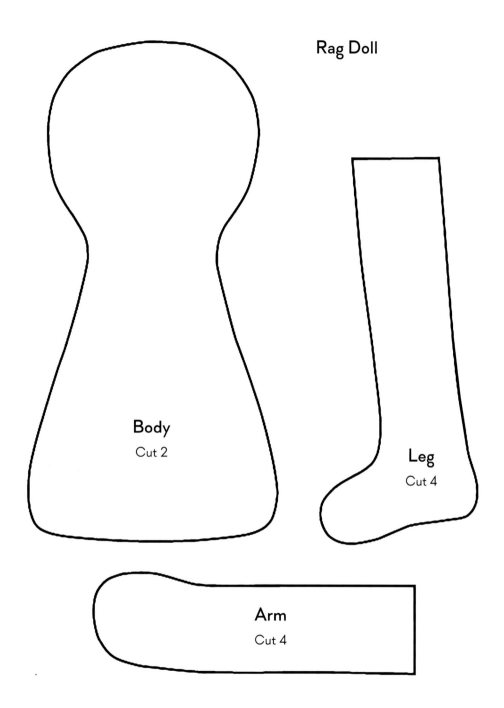

Rag Doll

Body

Cut 2

Leg

Cut 4

Arm

Cut 4

Editor: Meredith A. Clark
Designer: Darilyn Lowe Carnes
Managing Editor: Glenn Ramirez
Production Manager: Kathleen Gaffney

Library of Congress Control Number: 2021946824

ISBN: 978-1-4197-5484-5
eISBN: 978-1-64700-303-6

Printed and bound in China
10 9 8 7 6 5 4 3 2 1

Abrams books are available at special discounts when purchased in quantity
for premiums and promotions as well as fundraising or educational use.
Special editions can also be created to specification. For details, contact
specialsales@abramsbooks.com or the address below.

Abrams® is a registered trademark of Harry N. Abrams, Inc.

ABRAMS The Art of Books
195 Broadway, New York, NY 10007
abramsbooks.com